AF871497

Gail Bell was born in Sydney, is a graduate in pharmacy and education from the University of Sydney, and has worked in Australia and England. Her travel writing, book reviews, critical essays and long-form journalism have won acclaim and prizes. She is the author of two books, *The Poison Principle* and *Being Shot*, and a *Quarterly Essay 'The Worried Well'*. She lives on the NSW Central Coast.

gail-bell.com
facebook.com/gailbellonline
twitter.com/hemlockgreen

Praise for *Being Shot* by Gail Bell

'[A] public service as well as a work of art. [Its] prose has an exquisite precision.' *The Age*

'If *The Poison Principle*'s greatest gift was its willingness to provide a widely digestible understanding of science to its readers, then *Being Shot* will surely deliver one of the most honest and compassionate discussions of grieving to be printed in Australia.' *The Courier-Mail*

'Far from gloomy or academic, this is a riveting and uplifting read, a book that is gracefully and stylishly written.' *The Canberra Times*

'... a searing, personally resonant examination of Australia's relationship with guns, with a similar gut-impact to Michael Moore's documentary film on the US experience, *Bowling for Columbine*.' *Bookseller + Publisher*

'Bell writes superbly. Spare, precise, yet evocative.' *The Weekend Australian*

'... an impressive encore from an author who won the NSW Premier's Literary Award ... extraordinary and engrossing.' *The Sydney Morning Herald*

'... a visceral, compelling, and fascinating book.' *The Sunday Telegraph*

'... Bell's fine writing skills have turned an unusual topic into an interesting, lively and absorbing piece of storytelling that never flags for a minute and will appeal to a large audience.' *Australian Women's Weekly*

BEING SHOT

GAIL BELL

BRIO

b
BRIO

Published by Brio Books in 2018

Brio Books Pty Ltd
PO Box Q324, QVB Post Office,
NSW 1230, Australia

www.briobooks.com.au

First published as *SHOT* by Pan Macmillan in 2003

ISBN 978-1-925589-16-0 (print)
ISBN 978-1-925589-17-7 (digital)

All rights reserved. Without limiting the rights under copyright below, no part of this publication shall be reproduced, stored in or introduced into a retrieval system, or transmitted in any form or by any means (electronic, mechanical, photocopying, recording or otherwise), without the prior permission of both the copyright holder and the publisher.

The moral rights of the author have been asserted.

Text copyright © Gail Bell 2003, 2018
Cover and internal design and typesetting copyright © Brio Books 2018

Cataloguing-in-publication data is available from the National Library of Australia

Cover design by Xou Creative, www.xoucreative.com.au
Printed and bound in Australia by McPherson's Printing Group

Papers used by Brio Books are natural, recyclable products made from wood grown in sustainable forests. The manufacturing processes conform to the environmental regulations of the country of origin.

For my mother,
Alice Charlotte Asquith
1928–2016

Some names have been changed to protect individuals and safeguard against future proceedings.

Author's Note

For a few months in 1968 I was that girl in the newspapers who was 'scared to walk the streets alone'. The TV news gave updates on my recovery. Reporters camped on the front lawn. There was nothing special about me, other than my youth and my misfortune on that night, certainly nothing approaching the shock assassination of Martin Luther King Jr earlier that same month or the rising casualty rates in the sixth year of the Vietnam War. And yet, there seemed to be a strong appetite for ongoing reports about a girl from an out-of-the-way town who had walked into the darkness and been shot.

In 2003 I wrote *SHOT*, a book that returns to the night of my shooting then broadens its reach into Australia's growing gun culture. I worked with the data that was available then and followed the developing research into post traumatic stress disorder (the diagnostic criteria for which were still evolving). In the decade and more since then, firearms offences have risen sharply. A non-fatal shooting such as mine might still be noticed, but it would not incite a new and troubling sense that random danger was abroad in a suburban street close to you. That message is well understood in 2018.

The content of the book stands exactly as it was, only the title has been altered slightly to reflect my original concept of presenting a 'personal response to guns and trauma'.

Being Shot is a narrative time capsule, a book about a more innocent time and a girl who looked into the darkness of a new estate and saw only the shortcut to home.

My thanks to my agent Selwa Anthony for her ongoing support and to Rod Morrison of Brio Books for his enthusiasm at republishing this very personal book.

Part One

BODY MY HOUSE
MY HORSE MY HOUND
WHAT WILL I DO
WHEN YOU ARE FALLEN
May Swenson, 'Question' (*Nature: Poems Old and New*)

WHILE WALKING HOME one dry moonless night in 1968 I was shot in the back.

The experience was spectacularly new to me; I had nothing to compare it with, no neural circuitry to process similarities, no language for the shock.

When the bullet struck I travelled forward an extra half-step, as if someone wielding a broom handle had given me a rude shove from behind. One minute I'd been walking with intent (I was late), the next I was off balance, faltering towards a full stop.

After the shove-feeling came a cracking noise, a sine curve of sound, *kerwump*. Sensation and sound separated by milliseconds – shove, *kerwump*. To the startled brain, this procession of events has no meaning. My computer ran its checks of memory stores and drew a blank.

Soldiers who are primed for gun battle have told me that even in a state of highest combat alert, being shot still comes as a surprise. The body is lifted up or thrown sideways by some mad poltergeist, and it is only with the return of conscious awareness that comprehension takes over from confusion.

When realisation arrived for me it came hesitantly, like a messenger unsure of the address. I used up valuable and dangerous seconds trying to work out what had happened. The shooter, I saw, was in a car fifteen metres away. When that pulse of comprehension arrived, I turned and ran for my life.

—

I didn't see my attacker's face. I saw a car and a shape at the steering wheel, only as much as the eye will register when you swivel your neck and glance over your shoulder.

From the shooter's vantage point, the target was a tall girl walking northwards into the darkness.

He saw the back of me, I saw a glimpse of a shadow.

After the bang and before I ran – in that pause where visual contact might have been made but wasn't – the car remained ominously still.

Speculation about what he was doing is a luxury for later, for now. Then, I had no thought, only reactions. Now, I am harangued by questions: Was he re-loading? Was the gun jammed? Was he waiting to see if I would fall down dead? Was he playing a game with complexities I couldn't begin to imagine?

That pause was significant in other ways. For me it was the hiatus before an opera of panic and pain. For him, I can only guess. As I ran away, he revved the motor of his car, spun gravel and sped out of sight. I almost wrote 'he gunned the car', but it was me, the girl in the new maroon shoes, he gunned.

—

The thirtieth of April 1968 was, according to records, a clear sunny day in Sydney. April is an autumn month in the southern hemisphere, a sweet respite from the heat, cicadas, bushfires and suntan lotion of an east-coast summer.

I know exactly what I was wearing on that evening from a police receipt for 'items held for examination'.

1 x blue wool-blend fully-lined skirt
1 x maroon Bonds ribbed t-shirt with long sleeves
1 x petticoat, bra, step-ins, panties, stockings
1 x cream-coloured cardigan, cable knit, with collar
1 x pair maroon shoes

It is extraordinary to me to possess these details. When I read the list now I can re-inhabit those pieces instantly, as if I stepped out of them this morning. The skirt, for instance, had pinstripes and was part of a suit with a matching jacket that I made at home under my mother's supervision and was (therefore) never short enough for my liking.

Later, the cardigan and top and petticoat would be discarded – for reasons of tidiness, moving on, forgetting; not to mention a crusty black accretion of something organic around the hole in each. The shoes I wore for another season, then threw off a bridge.

I can reconstruct the day of the thirtieth itself, not in isolation (that would suggest omens or forebodings, and there were none) but out of the sameness of all those days when I was living in the western suburbs and taking a daily train to Wynyard (two stops past Sydney Central) to my job as a clerk at the Totalisator Agency Board, an off-course betting authority (established by the government in 1964, now privatised) with city and regional branches, and known to punters, still, as the TAB.

In my statement to police I said, 'After work I changed out of my uniform and caught the bus down George Street to Ultimo, then walked along Harris Street as far as Mary Ann Street to go to my chemistry class.'

In 1968 I aspired to be a laboratory assistant and had enrolled in a two-year part-time Certificate course at Technical College. My chem class always finished on time, at 8 pm on Tuesdays. After packing up I stood around with a few classmates, lamenting something or other – the lack of time for study, the long days, the assignments – while I waited for my new and special friend, Margot, to give the nod that we were ready to leave.

Margot was part of my other life, the one lived parallel to my clerking days at the TAB. In Margot's company I was under-studying the role I planned for my adult career, part well-groomed scientist, part poet, and part Grace Kelly in *High Society*.

Margot worked in a laboratory. She spent her days looking down a microscope at the aquarium world of blood cells. Her job was to spot the rogue swimmers, the misshapen interlopers prowling the waters, and call attention to their presence. She was groomed and classy and had a semi-tragic background (mother dead; father lost to grief, working mad hours), and I adored her chic take on the world. I was toning down my make-up (excessive sixties eyeliner and thick foundation) in homage to her clean honey-coloured skin. She once drove me to the gates of her house in an exclusive part of Sydney, but no further. Explaining why I couldn't enter didn't occur to Margot. Our class differences were taken for granted, or so my limited experience of inscrutable rich girls interpreted it. Just below the surface of everything she said or did lay the sadness of her mother's death and the unbridgeable distance between someone in grief and someone who is not.

Margot was older and she had a car. Our leave-taking was always abrupt and rather regal; she disdained small talk and my tic of giving running commentary – 'I'm just putting these test tubes in the rack', and 'See you on Thursday everyone, we're leaving now'. This self-evident amplification was left hanging in the air as Margot sailed past the other students, one hand in her coat pocket (the hand holding the car keys), the other held out in front of her like a baton in the resting position. Nothing was ever said until we'd settled in the car and she'd inserted but not turned the ignition key. I have no recollection of what we talked about, and no inkling of what my contribution could have signified, only the sense that she wanted some company and I was better than nothing at the time.

After, and sometimes during, the talk in the car Margot would fall into a sort of reverie, as if something she had long suspected was being confirmed before her eyes. It was a mannerism I tried to copy in other places, at home or at the TAB. I think now that reverie is the foundation of change and have developed my own ways of withdrawing from the onslaught of chatter and opinions, but then, in my apprenticeship, any staring into space quickly became the target of snapping fingers.

Margot's car would pull up opposite the entrance to the underground tunnel on Broadway, I would leap out without a backward glance ('that unnecessary gesture') and half-walk, half-run through the tunnel, up the flight of cement steps, down onto the platform and into my train carriage in an adrenaline haze of purpose and belonging.

Only, on this night, this life-changing night, something went wrong. Margot didn't come to chem class and I missed my train.

—

Margot plays no further part in this narrative except as a diary entry. Like a proficient usherette from a fifties cinema, she wields her torch beam until all are safely seated, then vanishes with the light. After that evening and my long absence in recuperation, we grew apart. Whatever we were building between us didn't survive the wrench of my being pulled into what must have seemed to her a consequence of western suburbs bloodlines. Losing Margot marooned me in a place between worlds. Given a little more time I might have acquired some of her gloss, or learnt how to create a little shine of my own, but as it happened, I was struck down before any metamorphosis had taken hold. This is not revisionist vanity. Quite a lot was made of the fact that I was a girl from Toongabbie, then a suburb far enough west of the GPO to qualify as 'the sticks', a landscape construed by the class-conscious as beyond the pale of sophisticated living.

—

It was 10.10 pm when the late train reached my stop. I was the only person to get out. No ticket collector appeared from the locked but lighted office, no spectral faces looked out at me from the carriage windows. It is tempting to play up the Gothic omens of that evening – the lack of moon, the echoing noise my shoes made, the looming shadows beyond the street lights – but even if they register now, they didn't then. The train had deposited me on the safe shores of my home town, a landscape engraved in my memory – as all our childhood landscapes are – so that I can close my eyes now and still bring to mind every street and house.

Facing the station was a strip of shops. The extra lighting at the pedestrian crossing lit up their blank windows and closed doors. Paul's Milk Bar. The Bric a Brac Shop. The grimy mysteries of the Auto Electrician's.

I stood across from the shops, under the light, waiting for my father. He came to meet me on class nights, twice a week, an arrangement I took for granted but which I now know interrupted one of his favourite wind-down activities, watching all-star wrestling on TV. My father worked twelve hours a day, often six days a week. In 1968 he was forty-one, had five children, and although physically strong and almost supernaturally good-natured, he exhibited obvious symptoms of longstanding fatigue.

I was going through the night's events as I waited – the long walk from my evening class to Central railway, missing the train, taking the next one, a Liverpool suburban that branched off my line at Granville, how I got out at Granville and how, miraculously, I transferred to a Penrith suburban just setting out on its westbound all-stops trip. It was complicated, and probably not what he wanted to hear, but my underlying message, *it's not my fault I'm late*, might carry more weight if delivered, as it were, in a storm of mitigating circumstances. As the minutes passed with not a single car coming by in either direction, it dawned on me that my father had no way of knowing I'd lucked onto an intermediate timetable; having already made the trip to the station once he wouldn't be here again for another thirty minutes, the scheduled time for the next ex-city train.

However these things are arranged, how the timing gets scrambled is part of the mystery of that night. We had no telephone in 1968.

With all the bravado of a girl in charge of her destiny, I crossed over the road and struck out through the short-cut.

—

Viewed from the overhead foot-ramp of the railway station, the short-cut at night was a bowl of darkness cut by a string of three streetlights, its only sign of life the new fire station, a square utilitarian building that laid an envelope of yellowish light across the empty road. At the outermost edge of the bowl you could just make out the return loop of the long-way-around, the safe road that led to home.

To reach the new estate road I crossed an empty block, using the fire station as a marker buoy, though I could, I believe, have made that journey blindfolded. When I stepped off the grass onto the road, I paused to run a finger along the tight seam at the back of one of the new shoes I was breaking in. As I straightened I shifted my load of books and launched myself into the ten-minute hike home.

With that first step onto the road I heard an ignition key turn and a car engine fire quietly into life. I could place the sound exactly, it was behind me and to the left, somewhere in the bank of darkness behind the hardware shop. A car must have been parked in the private access lane leading to the back entrance. In the pin-drop quietness the acoustics expanded and separated into components. I clearly heard the note of a gear box shifting from idle to first gear.

My ear tracked the sound, a sound like a dog waking up, shaking itself, giving a small growl; then the slow roll of rubber on blue metal, the stealthy crunching undergrowth sound of something prowling.

The hunger I'd been feeling seconds before vanished. My sore feet healed. The biting weight of books in my tote bag was lifted up and away by fairies. My heart roused itself from slow march to double-time. It's quite possible that the small hairs on my neck stood to attention.

I peopled the car with boys. Boys gathered together for the purpose of rape – a gathering I'd been warned about as long as I could remember. I imagined them, passing around a bottle, inhibition boundaries met and crossed, stripped back to their most primitive manifestation by vodka and urgency. I looked around for someone to scream to, and knew, tragically, self-pityingly, that I had chosen the wrong way home.

My instinct was to ditch my bag and shoes, get off the road and run like hell to the creek. If I hit the ground and rolled I could disappear down the creek wall and scramble up a slope into the bush.

I eased my bag off my shoulder, and brought it to rest against my abdomen as I increased my walking speed. I made ground, extending the distance between myself and the car. I was winning. Two more steps and I'd be level with the fire station and its warm light. Behind me, the crunching stopped.

I couldn't know that a bag of books slung low on the back makes a good shield, just as I couldn't know the driver was playing a different game. Where I was playing 'chase', he was playing 'aim'. By advancing into the blanket of light thrown on the road by the fire station I had taken myself from a low-vision field right into a shooting gallery backdrop.

My body entered the light at the same time as I sensed a different agenda. I stopped and turned my head, rotating my upper body enough to see what was behind me.

—

The bullet that whacked into my back went almost through to the other side. The entry point was an inch to the left of my spine. All my life since that night (and maybe before, but I wasn't paying attention then), if some part of me is injured it happens on the left side. If that speaks of a pattern I'm curious to know its meaning.

The body sensation was blunt. There was no perception of sharpness, nothing seemed to tear open.

A low-velocity solid lead bullet tends to bore straight through whatever's in its path, losing energy as it moves along the wound track. As it travels, it crushes and tears tissue, creating a cone-shaped cavity that narrows down as the bullet slows. My bullet ground to a halt beneath a rib, like a runner who sprints the last yards to the boundary fence then leans on the barrier, done in.

In its path were organs it might have punctured. Luckily (freakishly, the surgeon said), it merely skimmed the outer membranes, flicked away like a pinball by some god of chance who was on the case that day. Five years after the shooting, when the original decision to leave the bullet where it lay was overturned, a surgeon who was searching my insides first saw the anatomical damage. He could see, he told me after the operation, exactly where the missile had tunnelled through. I tried to imagine how it would look. I wondered how the slippery loops and tubes could hold a shape for so long. It made me think of a wet forest where robust growth gathers in broken branches, tangled vines, and knits them back into the vegetal pattern, and where, yet, with patience you can still discern an old path in the undergrowth.

—

The place I ran to after I realised I'd been shot was the fire station. There was no other destination in that dark subdivision that gave any hint of light or habitation, and I was only a few yards from its door.

Recently I retraced my steps to the place I was shot, stopping in front of the fire station that had been my sanctuary, to see if its shape and dimensions accorded with my memory, and was confused to find the building converted into a bungalow. The conversion evoked a cold rage in me that took a few weeks to work through. It had something to do with that red, square-fronted public building being transformed into someone's private if odd-looking house.

The entrance path ran up the side in 1968 (and still does), and through the open slats of a venetian blind I saw a man inside. He had one buttock resting on the edge of a desk and was swinging his leg as he spoke into a telephone. I banged my fist on the locked door. When nothing happened I moved back to the window to show the man my face, improvising a pantomime, using my grimace and pleading muscles, attempting both to alert him to my plight and to reassure him that I was genuine – not dangerous, not mad. When he showed me a querying frown I beat harder on the glass, pounding a mayday of dashes and dots that left him no option but to open the door a cautious inch, enough for me to bowl past him like an interstate lorry, banging him with my tote bag, spinning him in my slipstream. This man, whom I never saw again, this fireman on the graveyard shift sitting out the long hours, became in an instant that most sought-after specimen, my rescuer. The telephone, still connected, lay where he had placed it.

In an interview with a Sydney newspaper, the fireman told a reporter: 'She said: "I've been shot, I've been shot."' If this is correct, and I have no reason to doubt the report, it means that in the few minutes since *shove/kerwump* I had made sense of the madness outside. I'd named the assault and was creating within me and around me a context for remedial action.

The fireman, torn, I suspect, between receiving and evicting me, put his hand to my back in a guiding motion, indicating a chair, and then – as if stung – snatched his hand away. We saw the blood at the same time. We stared at the outrageous redness of it then locked frightened eyes on each other. The shock sent him straight to the telephone to cancel his caller and flipped him, like a quick-change artist, into his professional persona, the trained expert with procedures and experience to consult and act on.

I sat in his chair watching him tear off a paper towel to wipe his dialling finger, my world contracting into pain as his expanded into the role he was born for, his adrenaline pumping, his brain quick-thinking its way to solutions.

I was reduced to one sustaining thought: *this room is our fortress, we're in this together now*.

Pain, real pain, was an experience I knew little of before that night. Sitting in his chair, surrendering, I let go of the imperatives of escape and refuge. My goals were attained. I couldn't think of anything else to do. I sat like an animal, hit but not killed by a passing car. And into the void left by imperatives crept pain, the visceral response to trauma. The dull amorphous ache that had begun as I came through the door sharpened its outlines to become an entity like a heavy weight laid at an awkward angle across my spine.

The fireman gave me something to drink from his first aid kit. I watched him measure drops into a glass of water. I don't know if the drink or his gentle manner calmed me out of my agitation; what I began to feel was an altered communion with pain, as if the battle of severed nerve endings had paused for breath. The opium, I later learnt, steps in like a chaperone to keep pain at a respectful distance.

After some time an ambulance arrived. Then a police car. Then a detective in a suit. Male voices contended in the airspace above my head. From what seemed to be a faraway place I listened to them debate matters of priority.

'She has to be stretchered.'

'I need to ask a few questions first.'

I wanted someone to go to my house and tell my parents. I fixated on my request, making it over and over. 'We haven't got a telephone,' I explained.

At the open doors of the ambulance, lying on my back, I remember looking upwards at where the sky would be if there were any light up there. I had a strange, slightly excited feeling that everything was going to be alright; it was the merest flash of luminescence, like the twinkle in a fortune teller's eye, like something you want to believe despite evidence to the contrary.

Just as the stretcher jolted against the ambulance tray, the detective leant over me. He had a thin face and dark brown, acorn eyes. He asked me to describe the car.

Not then and not now do I have an eye for cars. I'm

not interested enough to retain the shape-memories in my brain. I knew the easy ones – the VW Beetle, the Mini, I knew convertible sports cars had no top, but the rest were a fairly amorphous group of conveyances to me. The detective, barely hiding his annoyance, humoured me with a process of elimination. He ticked off on his fingers – a truck? a utility? a panel van? I said yes to a sedan. I said it was two-tone because I couldn't remember the colour. The truth was I didn't register the colour, I saw 'a car'. I said I thought it was, maybe, a Holden, maybe an EH.

My father drove a two-tone EH Holden. I had reached into my small deck of car knowledge and extracted an ace. The detective wrote a note. I was off the hook.

I was lifted into the ambulance and driven at high speed to the nearest hospital.

—

This is what my memory can surrender about those first hours in hospital. It is not everything that happened. The fragments that materialise arrive fresh – minted in another time yet vivid with the intensity of now – and wrapped in a luminescent cellophane of feeling.

For instance.

The young doctor who smelled of minced beef and onions and had large frightened eyes. The nurse who took over when he couldn't get the intravenous line in and working. The sense that my siren-wailing entrance had disturbed a pre-existing atmosphere of unthreatening routine. A blood pressure cuff. The sting of a needle. The clatter of metal instruments.

The blanks in between are punctuated by a sense (remembered and recreated by the remembering) of people doing a job but at the same time trying to put their own stamp on a communal effort. What my father might have termed 'too many chiefs'. Or a movie set where everyone is a director and no one wants to paint the scenery.

The procedure to insert an IV line hurt and took far too long. Up to this point I hadn't shed a tear but I began to feel the stirrings of a babyish whimper.

When the line finally worked I was wheeled into another room under very bright lights and lifted onto an examination table. Either then or some time soon after, the rest of my clothes were removed and a great deal of attention was given to looking for an exit wound. A senior medical officer had been called out of his bed to assess and direct. He was a man probably the age I am now. His manner was efficient, detached, watchful. For someone so recently roused from sleep he showed no signs of slowed mental processes. He ordered a shot of narcotic pain relief that, on top of the laudanum, improved my mood enormously.

I remember white sheets, bright lights, busyness, a sense of open space, a clean and friendly new land where vertical people were engaged with the needs of the recumbent. I was from the horizontal tribe, a wounded stranger en route to an uncertain fate.

What is vivid and etched for me was the sudden arrival (like my peep at the night sky) of a deep sense of self-awareness – a neuronal manifestation, the sort that makes us conscious animals – the sense that I was *alive*. And having it confirmed by experts meant that nothing that came afterwards, no amount of vexation, could subtract from the intoxicating high of surviving. Like a pair of glittering eyes that suddenly break the black canvas of a television cartoon night, the thing that was me materialised; sentient, knowing, *there*.

—

Later, coming out of a doze, I looked up to discover the anxious faces of my parents, very close together, mirroring each other's expression of frantic concern. I imagined them once looking at me that way over the edge of a cot, worrying if my rash was scarlet fever. This was a look to drown in, to absorb greedily in a selfish infantile way, and I gazed back at them from some faraway cradled place.

When we spoke it was tender and private. *Are you alright? Yes, I'm alright*. Nothing momentous, just the simple connecting threads we'd been spinning backwards and forwards between us all my life.

They told me that two uniformed officers had come to the door, asked them if they had a daughter named Gail, then, almost matter of factly, said I'd been shot. No words of comfort, no extra details that might soften the blow.

Our moment of intimacy was usurped by a doctor ordering X-rays. My parents stepped aside as I was wheeled away, and from my view on the trolley I watched my mother put her head on my father's shoulder as if to say *she looks worse than we thought*, inciting a desire in me to shout down the hallway, *no, it's just shock, you're only seeing the surface, everything's fine, please, don't worry*.

Trundling along the corridor I began to feel more awake, partly from willing myself to look more alert for my parents' sake, and partly because I was cold. My clothes were gone and I was in a gown that was inches too short for my long body. A wardsman pushed me into the X-ray room, passed on instructions to the technician, then disappeared, leaving me with a new man in a white coat. When I tugged at the thin blanket for warmth, he whisked it away. He was older, solid, chunky, and he gave me an instant case of the creeps. As the blanket came away I lay revealed in my inadequate gown. If I shifted my shoulders, my upper thighs rode into view, if I inhaled deeply I showed my pubic hair. There seemed to be no way to hide myself. Without once taking his eyes off my lower body, the man indicated the position he needed me to assume for the photographs. These, I realised, were being taken by someone else, someone off stage who was setting things up and was relying on the technician to prepare the patient.

It seems curious now to think that the pervy stare of a sad and probably sick man precipitated an hysterical attack in me, where not an hour and a half before I had barely flinched after being shot in the back – but loud and hysterical is what I became in that windowless, crypt-like room, naked in front of two men, served up on a table like a sacrificial virgin. I screamed the place down. My back-opening gown had twisted under me, and I could see, even as I cried out, the man's sly dirty eyes all over me like some hairy spider running for cover. I swore. I cried big wet tears. And I demanded he be sent away.

The invisible radiographer suddenly manifested himself and a female nurse was called to the rescue. The nurse dealt with the blood coming from my wound and, in an act of humanity, draped my body below the waist with a second gown. I don't know what happened to the man who had been ejected by my wailing. At the time I hoped he'd crawled off somewhere to die. I wanted rats to bite off his nose and cockroaches to tunnel through his eardrums. I balled up the rage in me and aimed it at him like a missile, like (I now realise) a bullet. At seventeen I didn't know any psychological theory. I was pure wounded child.

DURING THE X-RAYS I experienced a sickening, searing pain that took my breath away. Deep in my body there was another kind of protest going on, one that responded to underground messages and feedback, like a bombed city shifting its rubble after a series of collapses. The pain tunnelled through me, leaving an afterburn of solid lingering hurt. And my mind jumped around, arriving at frightening conclusions. Maybe I wasn't as unscathed as I first thought, maybe these were my last minutes alive and I didn't even know it. The hopeful way my parents let me go might have been staged to send me on my way happy. The nurse with the pale grey eyes might have been sent to wrap my body for the morgue.

I remember this brief dance with paranoia very clearly. It was the first intimation that my injury might be bigger than my determination to dominate it.

—

Back in the unit I snapped out of my panic attack. Surrounded by familiar objects and staff I remembered from before the X-rays, I calmed down enough to make a joke. My parents looked so lost I said, thinking it would introduce a lighter note, 'Dad, I know I can annoy you sometimes, but really ...'

I said this with a broad smile, the way comedians deliver a punchline. I looked from face to face waiting for the laugh that would crack open the wall of deep concern that seemed to be leaning on top of me, cutting off my oxygen.

What happened next still dismays me. I can feel my face colour at the memory, an orphan blush left over from a time long ago when my big mouth caused someone I loved to suffer a public indignity.

The detective, who had never been far away, made his excuses to the doctor – who had apparently been struck dumb by my joke – and led my father to a quiet end of the room. I saw a flash of fright in my mother's eyes and knew instantly that I'd done something incredibly stupid. My father had been pulled away from our safe inner circle and re-positioned on the receiving end of an interrogation to establish an alibi. It was the biggest joke of all. Surely the detective couldn't be serious. Surely a trained investigator could spot a quip, even one in bad taste, and see it for what it was. I turned my head to stare at another transit passenger lining up for attention. A metal worker or mechanic by the look of his navy blue overalls. Something had made a fearsome mess of his arm. My sense of humour rolled over and died.

—

Lying in intensive care, moored by plastic tubing to machines, I felt as if I was underwater, a highly charged state that combined sensations of comfort and buoyancy. It was the early hours of the morning and I could hear quiet voices at the nurses' work station that looked like the deck of a modern ship, curved, alive with screens, beeping softly like a mechanical pulse. I counted five other beds.

I had no curiosity about the silent figures under those white sheets; the natives of this sombre city seemed to be sleeping, if not peacefully, at least in easy reach of help. I should have been sleeping too in this safest of places.

Every aid to sleep was at hand, except perhaps the familiar dimensions of my own bed and the proximity of my family. Instead I worked hard at not closing my eyes.

The protective coating I'd lived in and with for seventeen years had cracked wide open. I was now engaged in the serious business of staying alive.

—

At 6 am the morning after the shooting, several reporters knocked at the front door of our house, rousing my sister Kerry, who at sixteen had been left in charge while my parents sat vigil outside the swinging doors of the ER.

My brothers, fourteen and nine, who shared a bedroom, woke up but were told to keep out of the way. My youngest sister, twelve, didn't hear a thing in her single room at the back of the house.

The reporters wanted a photograph. I long ago forgave my sister for the photograph she handed over. I understand the circumstances – fear, surprise, sleep deprivation, and the pressure to produce a recent black and white snap when you're not sure what's available or where they're kept and you're sixteen years old and shy – but to choose one of me in Cilla Black bangs posing as a drunkard at Luna Park was (to my teenage vanity) salt in the wound. My first words to her when we finally saw each other again were 'How *could* you?'

By the time my parents arrived home at 7 am our front lawn resembled a politician's press conference. My father, still angry from his alibi ordeal, had to field a volley of questions, as well as mystifying assertions, like 'gangland shooting' and 'revenge hit'. 'Just go home,' he said, 'that's what I'm doing.'

In an attempt to re-establish routine my mother packed my protesting siblings off to school via the side gate. Tired, distressed, disoriented, my parents closed the blinds and assumed a siege position.

—

At Blacktown Police Station 'the matter of Gail M' was receiving attention.

The detective in charge was the same age as my father and a veteran of tough cases. His best men were working on another matter, a murder at Pitt Town that was sucking the oxygen out of every other case on their books. Given that I was still breathing and expected to make a full recovery, my case was being treated as a 'shoot with intent', and the familiar protocols were already up and running.

I will call this man Detective Hamer. He is dead now. I went looking for him a few years too late, and instead located the detective, now retired, who had been transferred out of Blacktown to another station to coordinate the Pitt Town murder investigation. When we sat down to tea in his sunny house I found myself wishing he had been on my case all those years ago. He was a gentleman from another era with all the attributes that a life spent dealing fairly and honestly with some of the worst offenders in this land confer on a human being. He was fatherly, wise, and just slightly watchful, enough to let me see the cop he used to be when he was on big cases. It wasn't until our second meeting that I learnt how sensibly watchful he'd been. Apparently he'd had to float the possibility that I'd tracked him down to settle a thirty-year-old grudge. 'It happens,' he told me. 'But I fairly rapidly worked out that you were on the up and up.'

The reason I wished he'd been on my case was purely subjective. Detective Hamer didn't like me from the moment we locked eyes at the ambulance door. He made, I believe, some kind of judgment about me based on (if you believed the stories about him) the crime scene, or (as I believed) me personally. There was something about me that didn't conform to his reading of the parts to see the whole. The part I represented didn't fit. And he, being a policeman hooked on procedures, couldn't adjust his detecting lens to accommodate my inconsistencies.

—

To the objective eye my needs were being competently met by hospital care. I was rested, intact, hydrated, and healing. But deep in my body and mind things were not so tranquil. Stress hormones had left a trail of damage during the worst moments, substances I would learn the names of a few years later at university when I sat in lectures hearing about the endocrine response to trauma: cortisol, adrenaline, noradrenaline, vasopressin, oxytocin, the endogenous opioids. Glucose rushing to the aid of the immune system. We don't know, as lay people, how complex the interior battles can get.

In the space of a night, I'd crossed a divide between the safe lands of my youth and a previously unimagined world where a bullet can erupt out of nowhere, and half an inch measures the distance between good luck and paralysis, or death.

The shift was existential and irreversible.

Like breaking the surface after swimming underwater, or losing your balance on a wet diving board, I broke from one state to another, heart racing, breath pumping. Now I was wary and watchful, alive to every procedure, no matter how mundane, no matter how persuasively the medical staff tried to coerce me into mute compliance.

I became alert to sounds and whispers, half-sentences, nuances of tone, changes in grooming, pens moving across paper, clock faces, watches pinned to bosoms, the squeak of rubber on polished linoleum. I could smell what was arriving from the kitchen for those who could eat, and I knew what each nurse had for lunch, if she had her period, if she used hairspray before coming on shift, and who chewed Minties to disguise garlic or sherry breath. This hyper-awareness, this canine bristle, arrived on the wind like a visiting madness, and has stayed with me (in a modified form) most of my life since.

—

Against the possibility of abdominal sepsis I was given large doses of intramuscular streptomycin, another reason to stay on my guard. This injection, now rarely used, made me wince with pain, put a tingle on my tongue and giddied my head. Streptomycin has a narrow spectrum of action and these days is kept in reserve for unusual things like plague, rabbit fever, brucellosis, leprosy. The nurse with a sense of humour who liked to tie ribbons in my hair hoped it might clear up my acne.

I rarely saw a doctor. When I did, they came in multiples, to study my charts and discuss the unusual aspects of my case. I learnt, from listening in, that it was considered too dangerous to remove the bullet. Too many important organs close by. *Pax Romana*, one doctor said, a comment that mystified all except an old man in an adjacent bed who lifted his oxygen mask to painfully, breathlessly, sketch a verbal picture of Europe wherein small neighbouring countries maintained a peace of sorts with each other for fear of drawing the attention of a more powerful foe, the might of occupying Rome.

My rapid transition from everyday teenager to what the newspapers called 'a victim of violent crime' was something like a coronation. My street clothes were taken away, my body sponged and tinctured, and a semi-permeable zone imposed on my personal space. Only ladies-in-waiting could approach, only immediate family could speak, only

Detective Hamer – brooding like an embattled prime minister or lordly advisor – had my ear. Before the shooting, I was one thing; after, I became something else. Certain consequences follow from this kind of special treatment. The most personal and valuable is the sense of being taken care of by experts. I felt this immediately, and easily rose to the occasion, as most people would. It was like falling out of the sky into a safety net, with a caring audience waiting to pick you up and applaud your acrobatics. If I had known at the time how blessed and rare this safety net is, I might have valued it more. Others, I was to learn, are left to plummet to earth in a deathly, inhuman silence.

The hospital bed became a sanitised, regimented and relocated crime scene. I was the not-dead victim. My clothing and my story had become items of forensic interest that could be worked on elsewhere. But the bullet was the stopper, in more ways than one. The police needed the bullet, for obvious reasons. The doctors said it had to stay where it was. An impasse developed, leaving me in the uncomfortable, though largely helpless, situation of feeling both guilty for obstructing official investigations and grateful to the doctors for protecting my interests.

The police had very little to work with and only my word that I was alone and innocently unaware of my fate on that dark street on Tuesday night. And Detective Hamer, with his unhappy antelope face and five o'clock shadow, didn't believe me.

ON MY FIFTH DAY IN HOSPITAL I was sitting up, looking well, and reading the daily delivery of cards from well-wishers. The newspapers had made much of my case and many people had written messages, some in spidery writing, some beginning 'In my day, things like this were never heard of ...'

Over the top of my bed, the nurses put a sign: *World famous Daily Mirror star herself*. They tied my long hair to one side with hot-pink ribbon from one of the many bouquets that came each day. The atmosphere, no longer watchful, vigilant, stern, had lightened. We had moments of fun. And twice a day I walked with help along the corridor outside the ward, accommodating to a range of searingly painful sensations that twanged like snapping guitar strings in my back.

Hamer came most days for a short interview, updating his notebook, looking around, staying only minutes when I was really sick. The sight of me sitting up and smiling on this particular day seemed to disconcert him. He eyed the new setup warily then plunged into his questions, all roads inevitably leading to the car, always the car. Two-tone, I repeated. How was the colour distributed? He reminded me that my father drove a two-tone Holden EH, was it like that? And truthfully, honestly, I couldn't say.

He pointed to the get-well cards and asked if I'd been doing as he asked and putting to one side any card that seemed 'strange' or 'out of place'. Dutifully I'd made one pile of family, friends', work colleagues' cards, and another of unknowns. He took the second pile, which was large and had to be kept in a pillow slip, and began picking out random cards, reading aloud the messages.

Clearly the harem mood in the ward irritated him. Leaning in towards me, as if to impart a secret, he said, 'Today I'm going to sit here until you tell me who did it. It's as simple as that. I'm not moving until you stop playing games.'

This threat, finally verbalised, had been in his eyes for days. He looked purposefully at the pink bow in my hair as if it was a pagan symbol in a place of holy worship. He hated me. I was sure of it then, and also sure that he wanted the case solved so he wouldn't have to see me again.

I said what I'd said from the beginning: 'I don't know.'

He went back to sorting the cards.

'When did you live in Bondi?' he asked.

'I've never lived there,' I answered.

He read me a card in which the sender reminded me of the time we'd shared a house in that beach suburb. 'He wants to come and see you,' said the detective, tapping the card on his knee. I was still dealing with his attack on my integrity. My upbringing (and my age) predisposed me to accept a rebuke from the man in charge but Hamer's tone had pushed me too far. I rolled my head to the side and shut down. It was a classic 'go away' gesture, yet it had a surprising, almost paradoxical effect on his demeanour. He brought the card in line with my averted eyes.

'And see you he shall,' he said.

—

This sort of manoeuvre, I later learnt, is called a 'stake out'. Or was it a 'set up'? My detective had determined that the shooter, stricken with guilt, had written me a get-well card. This, he said, was common, or at least not unknown. I was moved to another ward, a small room with a nurse's desk, and two beds facing each other across an expanse of linoleum-covered floor. Propped up in the window bed, opposite two beds that were screened off, I was arranged like a mannequin, my head on the pillow, my arms at my side. Flowers and cards were carried from the other room and put into natural-looking placements on the small side table. There were different staff in here and they gave me wide-eyed looks as they obeyed the detective's instructions. I heard him ask a nurse if they should put a drip stand near my bed and she shook her head, saying, 'When they come to us they're off the drip.' She didn't understand that he meant the drip as a prop and he made a wry face. In my horizontal position I felt like a helpless infant put to bed when I wanted to play. From time to time the detective glared at me like a stern parent.

I lay there compliantly. Eventually the scene approximated what the detective had in mind. He stopped giving stage directions and called a number of people to join him at my bedside. Two men in white coats with doctor IDs turned out to be policemen in disguise. The real nurse (who wouldn't allow the drip stand) had been replaced by a policewoman in a nurse's uniform. Two o'clock was the appointed time for the shooter to visit. I was given a novel (a James A. Michener paperback) and told to pretend I was reading. Matters, I began to feel, were racing beyond my control. As the mute observer of this charade, I'd been enjoying the show; now I was propped up, once again like a target in a shooting gallery.

I could see holes in the arrangement. If the police could dress up as doctors and nurses, couldn't the shooter? I let a few scenarios play out in my mind. None of them pleased me.

'Two o'clock,' said the detective checking his watch.

I opened to the first page of *Hawaii*.

The pretend nurse wrote notes in a pretend nursing sheet and watched the doorway. The pretend doctors adjusted the screens around the empty beds and mumbled to each other. My detective walked up to the pretend nurse and gave her some more notes to copy.

I began to wish the gunman would burst in and spray the room with bullets, anything to break the tension.

'Master of life, guardian of the shorelines, regulator of the temperatures and heaving sculptor of mountains, the great ocean existed.' I wasn't getting very far with *Hawaii*.

I read the same line over and over again, then turned a page.

This charade went on for forty minutes. I wondered what was happening outside. Was there a marksman hiding in the laundry basket, was the normal business of the hospital still going on, had the world paused? I wondered if my parents knew (they didn't), I wondered if the hospital administration had given permission, and if we were taking up valuable space. I wondered about anything rather than entertain the idea I might be taken out by a sniper's bullet at any second.

We waited until 3 pm, then the detective suspended the operation. The pretend staff were stood down. I asked to go to the toilet and had to suffer the indignity of sliding onto a bedpan without curtains while the lawmen de-briefed in the doorway. Before leaving, the detective conferred with the real staff who were now reclaiming the ward. It appeared I was to be moved from this room to one of my own. Surveillance was to continue, with all visits screened. I was to keep sorting through cards and putting suspect ones to the side. The last thing the detective did before exiting was to shoot me a look of utter contempt, as if by failing to produce the perpetrator, I'd wasted even more of his valuable time.

—

Nineteen sixty-eight was the year I should have been still in high school, a girl among other girls in pressed tunics and white shirts, swotting for my final graduating certificate in a structured, collegiate atmosphere. Instead I was making up my life as I went along. Two days after my seventeenth birthday and six months before I was shot I had walked out of high school forever, setting fire to my exercise books, notes, and even parts of my uniform, in an anarchic and self-dramatising act to mark the end of dressing in navy blue serge with box pleats and the torture of keeping a hat (panama for summer, velour for winter) in presentable assembly-ground condition. The manifesto for my new life, had I written one, would have proclaimed my right to smoke in public, wear make-up, earn my own money and take my place beside a certain type of woman from my mother's generation – the hard-working post-war dames who could raise children with one hand and slip a new washer in the tap with the other. Before the 1960s I'd never met any 'new' or 'liberated' women. My mother's girlfriends wore crimson lipstick, polyester uniforms (usually blue), and when they arrived at our house – gasping for coffee – they slumped into a chair, lit up, and sucked on their cigarettes like survivors of some unspeakable horror. I loved what they did with their hair: the gravity-defying upsweep, the sculpting effect of curling rods, the helmet sheen of hairspray.

In our corner of the western suburbs of Sydney the revolutions of second-wave feminism, war protests and far-off political unrest were news items, ripples on the surface, never the tidal waves that upended a whole generation who lived closer to the edge. In the maelstrom of the sixties I watched my mother's girlfriends move out of curlers into perms and back out the other side to easy-care styles that would hold all day with one or two comb-throughs.

And as passionately as I desired membership in a sorority like theirs – and indeed found it in the pacy, tough-cookie life of the TAB – I was as confused as any teenager about the tribe I wanted to settle with. My dubious talent for entering a group, taking its measure and slipping into the pool with a minimal splash was acquired early and is an extension, for better or worse, of my immense curiosity about people and how they operate.

To complicate the mix, in my last months at school I'd been seduced by another kind of sisterhood, women who wore little or no lipstick and tucked poetry books under their arms on yard duty; these were the wise and intelligent women who taught at my high school and somehow saw through my hardboiled pose to depths I wouldn't believe were in my profile or destiny. From them I learnt about context. It is a huge leap for a mixed-up teenager to see a personal drama, like unrequited love or sibling rivalry, raised to another level through guided engagement with a text, and even if I scowled and affected boredom, I'd already begun (because of them) a journey away from my egocentric world view towards a grasp of the universal.

By day I wore my blue polyester TAB uniform, and by night I studied my way back into matriculation and onwards to a science degree. I don't think I was consciously playing off one group loyalty against the other, I was doing what came naturally, reaching beyond what I knew from childhood to what was on offer in the wider world; with two important (to me) differences between myself and everyone else who was doing the same thing. I was breaking free months before they did, and, even in transitional stage, no one could ever say I didn't pay attention to my make-up and hair.

—

I've always believed Hamer thought I was cheap. Even at seventeen I blonded my already fair hair. I wore a lot of eye make-up, a line of black on the upper and lower eye margins, and another line following the arch of the eye socket. The space in between I painted green or blue. It was peel-off eyeliner: I don't think it exists any more. At the end of the day you picked at a corner, lifted it and peeled it away like plastic paint, sometimes plucking out an eyelash or two if you weren't careful. I wore thick foundation to cover my pimples, and pink Bardot lipstick to give me pouty lips.

With his miss-nothing forensic stare, I figure that Hamer took one look at me and saw 'western suburbs trash walking alone at night asking for trouble'. Like a bad snapshot of your worst angle this first impression of me stayed with him, pinned forever to his board as exhibit A. I wanted results as much as he did, and to that end I tried to be a good witness to my own shooting. We just couldn't agree on emphasis. My focus was on staying well. I couldn't speculate in the way Hamer demanded of me. Speculation was beyond my post-shot repertoire. All my driving force was geared towards recovery and the future. Hamer probably didn't understand his attitude towards me himself. Maybe I resembled someone who'd given him a hard time on another case. Maybe he had a daughter at home whose rebel streak gave him heartburn. Or maybe, simply, our personalities clashed. He isn't here to put his case.

What is clear to me now is the great disservice he did me in not taking my youth, and my awkward half-this half-that personality, into his considerations and subsequent assessment.

His prejudice coloured all of his dealings with me, and led, I believe, to many of the misunderstandings and obstacles to progress that were to follow.

—

Meanwhile, my supporters brought gifts. From my high school teachers, Penguin Modern Classics, James Joyce, *Modern Poets 9* (Levertov, Rexroth, Williams), H.F. Ellis, and Faber's *Collected Poetry of T.S. Eliot.*

From the girls at the TAB, an oversize card with messages that bordered on the obscene – puns on the sexual connotation of aiming and shooting, taking it in the rear, and so on – alongside a box of Roses chocolates and a black garter belt to cheer me up.

Part Two

I TAPPED MY OWN HEAD;
IT WAS GLASS, AN INVERTED BOWL.
IT IS A SMALL THING
TO RAGE IN YOUR OWN BOWL.
Anne Sexton, 'For John, Who Begs Me Not To Enquire Further' (*Selected Poems*)

SHOT IS A NEAT, well-balanced word, its short vowel-sound as penetrating as the act itself, its meaning unambiguous in the right context.

When a victim is shot but not killed in the course of an assault or attempted murder, the crime is called 'shoot with intent'. In Australia the incidence of this sort of crime is very low: in 2000 it was 0.7 per 100,000 of population. In 1968 it was so unusual in Australia it rated front-page coverage. Seventy men and five women were killed by firearms in the whole of Australia in 1968.

Being shot propelled me, temporarily, into a hyper-real world peopled with policemen, doctors, nurses, journalists, photographers and, most unexpectedly, into the collective consciousness of Sydney citizens, who responded by sending me hundreds of cards and enough flowers to brighten an entire hospital.

The shooting and subsequent surgeries left scars that (thirty-odd years later) you would have to undress me to find. The original entry wound is almost invisible. The first surgery, an incision in the back that failed to locate the missile after several hours of probing, has left an elongated hyphen. The second and successful incision, below my left breast, is four inches across and more substantial – a testament to the surgeon's tenacity, and the application of rib spreaders.

But, until recently, I had yet to identify my mental scars. I had never wanted to be naked with them. I had barely allowed them to exist. They had become, through training and habit, as tightly corseted as a prim governess, and as inaccessible to seduction.

—

A body, once shot, is never the same again. It remembers what happened by storing its shock and outrage in unusual places: skin, muscle, connective tissue, nerves. Time passes, the body renews itself, but curiously, perversely, the visceral memory remains. Freud called this body memory 'physical fixation'. Pavlov described it as a cluster of defensive responses. How extreme this body neurosis or disturbance is seems to depend on the degree of insult to the body, and on the body's access to records of 'prior trauma' in the form of old memories; but the stand-out pre-disposing factors to not getting over physical assault seem to be related to how well supported the whole person perceives itself to be afterwards, and how well integrated the personality was to begin with.

—

There was an audience for my story as long as I chose to tell it (which wasn't very long), there were also the de facto blessings of those citizens who read my story in the newspaper and chose to write to me; and encompassing all of this was the strength of my family unit. Disorders of healing, or the prolongation of wounds and trauma, derive, the experts tell us, from a lack of listening on the part of one's community or family or colleagues, or the world in general, what Dr Jonathon Shay, in *Achilles in Vietnam: Combat Trauma and the Undoing of Character*, calls the 'communalization of the trauma – being able safely to tell the story to someone who is listening and who can be trusted to retell it truthfully to others in the community'.

Shooting is violence perpetrated from the outside, and

the body, caught unawares, has to muster its rescue teams in a hurry. A bullet wound is not like a disease that infiltrates by stealth and multiplies its armies by raiding the body's storage depots, at first pilfering, then escalating to robbery and siege. Neither is it a poison silently eating its host's vital centres. Being shot is a penetration experience. With all the connotations that evokes.

The response to trauma is complex and personal. Pavlov wrote that 'individual differences in temperament accounted for the diversity of long term adaptations to trauma'.

With some people the distressing symptoms fade over time. I have always felt that I belonged in this category of 'the healed', arrived there by an act of will, then later habituated to not thinking or talking about being shot.

The sister with whom I shared a bedroom in 1968 remembers me as 'changed' after I came home from hospital. Always a little highly strung, I became more 'jumpy' and 'irritable' than normal. I reacted to sudden loud noises. I slept badly, sometimes waking her up to fight off imagined prowlers, sometimes calling out words, more than once letting out a loud scream. I hated anyone coming up behind me; I slunk in my seat if a car pulled up level and cruised at the same speed as ours. My sister says this continued for the rest of that year, and though I have little or no memory of those behaviours in that time frame, it has to be said that all of them persist in me today in one mild form or another.

This prolongation of symptoms, over more than thirty years, speaks of some sort of brain recalcitrance over which my wilful self has had no control. None of the symptoms on their own is disabling. Even aggregated together they scarcely count for more than the profile of a 'nervy' woman who does a reasonable job of hiding her weaknesses. And yet we know from experiments with laboratory animals that prolonged stress causes damage somewhere in the body, usually in a place where we can't see or feel the exhaustion of defences. In the case of trauma, our bodies are dealing with a disordering of normal functioning. The adaptive changes that come into play after an assault of some kind are overwhelmed. Assault and the accompanying stress pose a threat to the steady state, and God knows what is going on in the secret cavities of our challenged (but not coping) anatomy. For instance, the adrenal cortex may be swelling while the thymus, spleen and lymph nodes might be shrinking. For all we know we might be softly bleeding from the linings of our stomach and duodenum.

The psychological damage is the part of the iceberg we see (or see expressed). Combat veterans who have survived the horrors of battle do more than cry out when a loud bang erupts. They dive to the floor, throw themselves off wharves, duck-roll under tables, reach for defensive weapons. Their version of not feeling comfortable when approached from behind converts to sitting only in corners that cover their backs.

—

Communalisation of my particular trauma was almost instant, thanks to the media. Seeing your story in print with photographs has a way of validating any doubts about what happened. In bold type, my story was being retold in a way that maximised sympathy for me and condemnation of the shooter, with no shades of grey, no equivocation about who was innocent and who was guilty. This is exactly what soldiers in distant Vietnam were missing out on. Their stories were sliding into oblivion almost as quickly as the action moved on to the next encounter, with no grace time for reflection.

I keep my clippings in a scrapbook. I've looked at them only a handful of times since 1968.

Beside a headline, *Who Could be so Callous to a Girl, 17*, and above the banner *SHOT DOWN FOR KICKS*, is a sombre-eyed girl staring directly at the camera.

The photograph memorialises me in that moment of my own drama, hurt but safe, conscious and responding to stimuli. My head is on a pillow set against the metal frame of a bed recognisable as standard hospital issue of the era. Only my face is on show. It emerges from sheets pulled up to my chin. My hair, longer and wavier then, is brushed to one side.

The weather on Thursday 2 May was dry with westerly winds. The *Daily Mirror* (a now-defunct afternoon tabloid with the 'biggest week-day sales in New South Wales') cost five cents.

Below my story is the beginning of another far more exotic international report. *The Boston Strangler. The Greatest Crime Story Ever Told.*

> On March 6th, 1965, Albert de Salvo alias the Boston Strangler, confessed to the murders of 13 women and girls. He also admitted to at least 300 attacks on other women. 'I'm tired of running,' he told the police, 'I want to get it off my chest.'

Attacks on women set the tone for the afternoon's reading. The lead story, my attack, is a shameless grab at the emotional sensibilities of evening commuters – a flashing beacon that signals changed conditions ahead – designed to lead the reader from speculation on who was attacking their own women (embodied by me) to the gruesome crimes of de Salvo, an expert in murder and mutilation.

My story began:

> In Sydney is a gunman who shoots for thrills. His victim, Gail M., shot in the back from a moving car as she walked alone down a street in Toongabbie.
>
> As she staggered into the fire station on Tuesday night, she

> gasped: 'I've been shot! I've been shot! Who would do a thing like that to me?'
>
> The car followed her from the railway station and the gunman stuck the rifle through the open window, fired one shot and wounded her.
>
> Miss M., of Fitzwilliam Rd., Toongabbie, is in Blacktown Hospital's intensive care ward with a .22 bullet in her back.

Looking at the photograph now I'm arrested by those eyes, that gaze. Then, it was direct, seeking, fearless, honest. My deep-set eyes are not in their caves here, not guarded, tense, ready to swerve sideways or down. Nowadays, only the aftermath of crying, or coming to the surface after holding my breath under water, will temporarily restore that gaze. I've killed it off over the years, a senseless murder perpetrated by someone striving for the opposite of innocence.

—

I've never tried to imagine the face of the man who shot me. My peace of mind depends too heavily on his anonymity. He is the watcher in the dark, the shape of a man in a car. Statistically, random shooting events are the trademark of eighteen-to-nineteen-year-old males. During a recent conversation with my father I quoted him the figures.

'I always thought it was a young bloke,' he said. 'Some kid mucking about with a Saturday night special.'

That's the thing about empty spaces, they invite all kinds of speculation. My father had his young hood theory; Hamer, after dismissing my father, turned on my new boyfriend; our neighbours upped the ante and conjured up a jilted lover rejected by a pregnant me; and when Ivan Milat was arrested for the backpacker murders, his penchant for shooting guns out of cars in my neighbourhood back in the 1960s was triumphantly brought to my attention.

None of it sticks. Whatever it is that helps me avoid a disabling stress disorder secretes a teflon coating at the mention of a breakthrough in the case.

The legacy I carry from that night is a changed appreciation of 'the dark'. My former happy relationship with the night hours was damaged by the stream of well-meant but disquieting warnings generated by those who sought to keep me safe. It seemed as if my parents' generation had all just read and taken to heart that line from *The Hound of the Baskervilles*: 'forbear from crossing the moor in those dark hours when the powers of evil are exalted.' Dark places, I was told, breed danger. Wolves, strangers, sex maniacs, thieves and slave traders apparently sat about waiting for seventeen-year-old girls to wander by.

And other changes arrived. Curfews. Reporting in (on our newly installed, priority granted telephone line). Chaperones. This is a form of torture to a gregarious spirit and one I chafed under.

Just before the shooting I'd started seeing an English boy. He wore round glasses like John Lennon, Carnaby Street clothes, and had an attitude. He got caught in the wash-up, was questioned, and initially seemed to enjoy the fuss – but his small measure of loyalty soon gave out. He dropped me.

After three months, in a follow-up story, the *Daily Mirror* showed me scowling at the camera on our front patio, under the heading *Scared to Walk the Streets Alone*, and indeed, at that time, I was.

—

Going home after so long in hospital felt flat and unreal. The flowers wilted, the cards got in the way of shared bedroom territorial lines, my brothers complained about curtailed freedoms because of my 'stupid bullet'.

My bed was underneath a window that faced, obliquely,

the main street. Traffic travelling west on Fitzwilliam Road made a constant hum we were all so used to we never heard, and yet I heard it now and was bothered by it. At night the headlights picked up the oblong of window light, cut in straight lines by the venetian blind, and lifted it in a mad race across the walls, enlarging and distorting its shape before dropping it back in its frame. I think my chronic insomnia began in those first few days home, watching the speeding shadow of spectral venetian blinds.

My mother had bought me a dressing gown, pink quilted, that covered me from neck to toe. There is a photograph on the third page of the *Daily Mirror* of me smiling above this frou-frou, with the headline *Bullet in Stomach for Life*.

Two representatives of the TAB head office arrived with a large box of Quality Street chocolates. I received them in my pink satin, demurely buttoned down to my slippers. Addressing my mother as the senior woman, they asked how long it would be before I returned to work. They were sympathetic, of course, but a job couldn't be kept open forever. My mother explained that the answer was up to the doctors, but she would keep them informed.

'They've got a nerve,' she said after she closed the door on them. I was five days over my sick leave entitlement for the year.

I was not encouraged, nor did I choose, to wallow. The mood around me was one of *cheer up, get over it*. After some more pressure from the TAB I went back to work, to take over the new telephone betting booth, because I was fast with figures and had a good telephone voice. My workmates were kind for a few weeks, then reverted to form. My best friend's mother suddenly died from a cerebral haemorrhage. Robert Kennedy was assassinated. My insomnia gave me headaches during the day and sudden noises made me jump but, like a broken arm, I was healing inside my plaster cast. Having survived, I'd planted my feet firmly on the path of wilful forgetting.

Gradually the newspapers lost interest, except for another follow-up story, *Girl Shot for Kicks Recovers*.

> Gail, according to police, is lucky to be alive today. The gunman was out to kill, they say. They believe he waited in a car near the station to shoot for thrills.

Hamer must have been the source of this quote, and I remember thinking that there was more information in those two or three sentences than in anything he'd ever told me.

In September I went to a dance in Parramatta and met the man I would marry three years later. One of the first things I told him about myself was that I'd been shot. It seemed to make me different, mysterious, deeper than other girls.

—

In his cross-examination of my report of what happened the night I was shot, Detective Hamer often tried to blame me for *encouraging* the crime. What in heaven's name was I thinking when I went for a stroll along a deserted street in the middle of nowhere on a pitch-black night? Was I trailing a neon sign that said Kidnap Me or Rape Me, or even better, Pull out a gun and shoot me? – no? Pity, a patrol car might have spotted me first and we wouldn't be having this conversation.

His tone snagged me, tugged me under like river weed, made me stumble. There was an answer to his question, just no compact, easy way to articulate it. The answer was a story about growing up, not a three-word reply, and I didn't have the confidence to move him away from his fast question-and-answer rhythm into my slower beginnings, middles and ends.

ON THAT NIGHT, I admit, I made an error of judgment. There were two ways home from the railway station, the long and the short. The long way followed the footpath that ran parallel to the main road. It was kerbed and guttered, well lit, and along its entire length was house after house belonging to families we knew or recognised or knew about, and into any of which I could have run for help and not been turned away.

The other way, the short-cut, was a blueprint for a new estate. I had grown up when the terrain was wild and so densely treed you could hide away forever and never be found. But in the late 1960s its great cathedral of trees had been felled and dragged off by developers. When Hamer saw the territory, every green thing had gone. It was a wasteland of new roads, scraped earth, and piles of bricks and timber waiting to be made into houses.

But our family had lived alongside the much older rural version of the landscape, the forested version, for ten years. We were creek children with a very physical appreciation of the locale and we'd played all over that wilderness long before it became Hamer's road-in-the-middle-of-nowhere.

For reasons I've written of elsewhere, my father had a confused, tenuous attachment to 'home', and when in 1957 our family expanded to four (later five) children he moved us to Toongabbie, a town that sits in a basin thirty kilometres inland from the east coast of Australia, directly west of Sydney.

There was a sense that everyone who landed in Toongabbie in the 1950s had been dropped there by accident on the way to somewhere better. For my parents it was a way-station, a house big enough for children, a chapter in a much longer novel. For us, the children, it was all there ever was, and we loved it.

We moved into an L-shaped fibro house on the corner of a main road. Directly opposite, across the bitumen, were wide green paddocks, becoming greener further back from the road where the ground was fed by a tributary of the Parramatta River called Toongabbie Creek. The creek ran roughly parallel to the main road, then turned at ninety degrees and cut the road two houses down from us at a place we called The Dip.

The men who lived around the creek were blue-collar workers, railwaymen, house painters, electricians, plumbers. In 1957 they wore rock-and-roll Brylcreemed hair, smoked hand-rolled cigarettes, left home before sunrise, had tribes of children and didn't go in much for socialising outside the moist tropics of the local pub. Most were ex-servicemen, some had escaped oppressive regimes in Europe, many had come across on migrant ships looking for a new start.

On Sundays the men mowed the grass, tightened things that were loose, and got about in shorts and singlets. The wives made their own clothes, cakes and biscuits, talked over the fence, wore aprons, always seemed to be doing something with pegs, allowed children an enormous amount of freedom, and demanded strict adherence only to being home in time for meals.

Living so close to a flooding creek meant that heavy rain could completely transform our landscape. The regular floods sent spiders floating in mad circles on leaf rafts, flushed out lizards and the occasional snake, left tidal lines on the paling fence and sometimes carried off boxes of papers and photographs stored below the waterline. The regular sluicing of what lived secretly under our house, which was on piers, was nothing however compared to the nights some foolhardy driver would accelerate through the tumbling water with a determination to beat the flood by sheer force of engine power and will.

These contenders rarely succeeded and we congregated at the front fence in nightclothes, watching the rescue attempts. My sister's friend from school, a lithe boy who was a good, strong swimmer, once volunteered to be tied to a rope and released into the current to do what he could for a floating car. We cheered ourselves hoarse.

The deeper parts of the creek fed a lush tree canopy where dark green vines hung like curled snakes and would sometimes hold the weight of a swinging child. Along the water's edge were mossy slopes and hollows made for hiding, or napping when the sun was high. We did our real swimming at the gleaming tiled pool a short train ride away and kept the creek like a place of secrets distinct from the supervision of watching adults.

My awareness of the landscape extended little further than a normal child's except in its acknowledgement of Toongabbie's convict history. My father's deep interest in the early exploring parties, his attachment to certain old eucalypts, and the expeditions we took to see the convict hanging tree and convict relics, all etched an impression of something darker beneath the safe, increasingly tamed terrain where we all lived and played. When Doris Sargeant, the mother of a boy in my class, wrote a history of the area, *The Toongabbie Story*, I found and underlined passages. An explorer, seeing the land for the first time, wrote in 1792:

> The hills in general are of good black earth. Both hills and vales are covered with trees of an amazing height and in many

> instances nine yards in circumference. They grow perfectly straight and nearly 100 feet high before the branches shoot off. [There are] large red and white gum-trees, oak, fir, mahogany, apple, pear, cherry.

Most of those trees vanished in a single six-week period some months after this same explorer's report, when Governor Phillip sent a supervisor and five hundred convicts to prepare the ground for planting. 'The wholesale destruction of the natural forest and the filling in of the natural course of the river and its tributaries' irrevocably altered a balanced ancient landscape.

When I learnt details, presented as tableaux by our school history teacher, of convicts yoked together like oxen pulling ploughs, living on small rations of salted meat and rice, emaciated, sunburned, bitten by snakes and spiders, terrorised by their overseers and dying at a rate of five per day, the relics took on a vivid meaningfulness that fed my interior sense that we were living in a strangely numinous place, although I would have not known the word or completely understood the concept. The deity I imagined was a destroyer, a Shiva of calculated subtractions.

By 1803 the prison farm at Toongabbie was abandoned and the remaining convicts relocated to a new penal holding in Castle Hill. Private land barons arrived, saw farming potential and began dividing up the spoils. 'Toongabbie had no official discovery in the true sense and no special announcement was made declaring it a centre' – an inauspicious beginning for a town with no happy memories, no founding fathers and too many references to the cruel treatment of convicts for anyone to feel the stirrings of community spirit.

—

Many of the streets near our house had Aboriginal names, most beginning with B, but in my twenty-odd years of living there I never saw an indigenous Australian. We encountered almost no one of colour except Mr Lowmow next door, who was half Chinese and had a honey-coloured tan so close to the summer colour of outdoor children as to be unremarkable. There were White Russians, Poles, Dutch, English, Greeks, Italians, Maltese – the acceptable face of migration in White Australia – scattered about in the 1950s. You had to get very close to the ground, follow the creek and read the land to recognise the footprints of the original owners. My sister and her friends knew a lip of sandstone that curled up like a small wave where there was primitive art etched into the rock.

The parcel of land that became the 'new estate' of my crime-scene statement once belonged to a family named Watson. The family lived in a cabin at the end of a dirt track. Trees, straight and tall as a building (the only stand of post-settlement old growth left), towered in a canopy over the underlying bush.

The frisson of fear I felt at playing on the Watson property owed a lot to its untamed bush, the sense of not knowing where the boundary fence was, and the way our games led us in and out of shadows and hidden thickets. Its riskiness was as far away as I could get from our quarter-acre of mowed grass with its paling fences, front and back yard, where every bit was known and named, and the mysteries had run out. Ours was a yard where my mother could glance up from her work and see, in one sweep, the chicken coop, the barbecue, the vegetable garden and the likely location of all five children.

Cutting through the western end of the Watson property was the original of the path we called the 'short-cut'. On a map from 1890 it is clearly shown as 'an old footpad track through briar and scrubs to the station'. Even in the nineteenth century it was quicker to cut through there than follow the longer way round on Wentworth Avenue.

When the Watson family sold up and the tractors came through like the convict teams to clear-fell, the people who lived along Fitzwilliam Road still trekked through the shorter way, ignoring the new grid lines, putting their feet on a public path that had been there since first settlement. Earlier this year I visited the 'new estate', now thirty-five years old, and walked the old route, stunned by the changes, a little disoriented by apartments that have gone up along the main road. At the northern end of the old path, where we used to cut through to Fitzwilliam Road and our house, they've made a park, which is bisected by a footpath. Sitting on a park bench, I watched a procession of people coming home from work. They'd emerged from the trains (now out of sight behind the two-storey apartments), crossed the street, cut through between the buildings, walked past the now-defunct fire station, down the road to the new park, past my bench, and emerged on Fitzwilliam Road, exactly the way we walked home all those years ago. Most of them don't know about the Watson family, or the long-gone, deep swimming holes that were once in the creek; they probably can't guess that this high-density settlement with its widened Fitzwilliam Road with no Dip (the creek was tamed years ago) was once a semi-rural backwater.

—

What was I doing on a road in the middle of nowhere, Detective Hamer? I was taking the short-cut home through the old Watson property. I was treading a path that had always been benign, familiar and safe. That something terrible happened has as little to do with my choice as a woman opening her umbrella in a sudden storm and being struck by lightning. Why open an umbrella? Because it was raining. Why walk home through the short-cut? Because it was quicker and I was late and it was just another Tuesday night.

PROJECTING ONE'S OWN lack of awareness of danger onto familiar surroundings is a common phenomenon in autobiographical writing. I later learnt from a retired detective that in 1968 there were twenty-seven murders in fourteen months in the greater Blacktown area (encompassing Toongabbie), and that two years after I was shot, two detectives were gunned down in Mimosa Avenue, a stone's throw from my arcadia.

Solving crimes is an imperfect science. The investigators arrive after the event when all that is left are physical traces and the recalled memories of witnesses and participants. Hamer, it seems to me now, was near to exhausting his small ration of leads. Without a bullet he couldn't bring in ballistics. Without witnesses he had a paucity of detail from other sources. I'm told by present-day police that the first thing they would do in a case like mine is haul in all the local gun nuts and ask them to account for their whereabouts. At the scene, they would look for tyre tracks, a spent cartridge, cigarette butts. If they had the manpower, they'd knock on doors and ask if anyone had heard a shot and an accelerating car. Then they'd probably start with the family and work outwards. One assumption would be that the shooter was known to me.

I'd given Hamer two names. One was Antonio, surname unknown, an Italian man who jumped out of his car one afternoon to introduce himself to me at the railway station. It was an extraordinary meeting. He was flustered and apologetic. He'd been watching me for a couple of days. He begged me to sit with him in his car, just to talk. I was a head taller than him and looking down I thought he had the loveliest eyes I'd seen, but I said no.

On the days I didn't go to evening class my train got in a bit after 6 pm and he was waiting at the same spot two days later. This time I stood with him for about five minutes. Being told you're beautiful is pretty hard for an ordinary teenager to resist. I noticed how cosy the interior of his car looked, like someone's favourite sitting room. Hanging from the rear-view mirror was a crucifix, rosary beads, and some amulets, maybe good luck charms. When I walked away he ran after me. On his mother's life, he said, he only wanted to talk.

The third and last time, I got into his car. He drove me without hesitation to within three houses of my home and parked in the side street. He was nervous. We had about ten minutes before I would get out and walk home as normal (it never occurred to me to think neighbours might be watching). In that time he proposed marriage. From the glove box he pulled out photographs of his family; his parents still in Italy, his brothers, one sister. Then he told me how utterly alone he was, how friendless, how lacking in love. He cried. I was young but I knew the difference between real and fake tears. I put my arms around him. He cried harder.

Telling Hamer, I felt like a rat. Hamer asked me what sort of car. I said it was small and white. He snapped shut his notebook. Here we go, I thought, I'm in for a lecture. Of course, I'd already heard it from my parents and the dobbing neighbour, and it's probably a lecture I would deliver now to a girl who put her trust in a stranger's hands, but I have an unshaken faith in Antonio's innocence.

The second name I gave was even harder to part with. Hamer had to work hard to get me in a talking mood. I had to tell him that the boy I used to date (and had been madly in love with) had gone to jail for stealing cars a few months before the shooting. Just the words 'stealing' and 'jail' seemed to implicate this former boyfriend (Hamer drew a circle around the new name in his notebook), but opportunity to commit the crime was (I thought) impossible from inside a prison – not to mention unlikely, knowing this young man as well as I did.

Hamer, however, discounted nothing and took down a list of places and dates.

—

If I had died on that night, I would have been seventeen years and eight months old, far too short a lifetime to know the world and its wonders.

By dying I would have missed a succession of milestones: my eighteenth and all subsequent birthdays, consummated sex, university, graduation, marriage, divorce, remarriage, nieces and nephews and the overcoming of acne. By the space of fourteen months I would have missed the first man on the moon. I would have died thinking Earth was all there was.

A lot of people would have cared that I'd gone, and mourned my passing, but the world would have kept turning. It always does.

—

Seven years ago my friend Jan lost her daughter Natalie when she was a month short of her seventeenth birthday. It was one of those vehicle accidents we call *senseless* because we can't think of a blameless, unloaded word. Three girls, high spirits, a new driver's licence begging to be used, a straight road, speed – and one of them dies. Jan's daughter. The back seat passenger.

The surviving girls are never sure of anything again.

At the graveside I watched the mother, rigid, uncomprehending; the father boned out, leaning on others; the sobbing schoolfriends with their single flowers to drop in the grave. I took my own frightening peek into that carpeted gateway to out-of-sight annihilation and felt the air pulled from my lungs.

We want to think that the universe is irreparably disturbed when a child dies. The chronology is wrong. The bewildered siblings, displaced in their natural order, have to reshuffle.

This could have happened in my family, I thought. My shy sister, fourteen months behind me, would have moved into the eldest sibling role. My youngest brother, nine years behind, what of him? Would I have left enough clues around for him to judge that, given time, I would have grown to love and respect him, when for the first nine years of his life I had treated him with either bossy overkill or silent disdain? And my youngest sister, Machele, who borrowed my clothes without asking and suffered my wrath, would she have ever guessed we would go to live on a farm in Holland one day and raise her daughter together in the ultimate playing out of harmonious sharing?

—

During the awkward period after Natalie's interment and the religious rites, when we stood around comforting each other, I looked over at a gardener mowing the lawn between graves. His offsider, a younger man, was weeding. They were in another world. I thought of but couldn't remember the opening lines of Auden's poem, 'Musée des Beaux Arts'. At home that evening I looked it up.

> About suffering they were never wrong,
> The Old Masters: how well they understood
> Its human position; how it takes place
> While someone else is eating or opening a window or just
> Walking dully along

In 1997 a friend who edits a small poetry magazine asked me to contribute a poem for a forthcoming issue called 'Shark at Charles Street Wharf'. The story behind the title was true and went like this: A large and dangerous shark had swum all the way from the Pacific Ocean along miles and miles of river to end up at a wharf in inland Parramatta. My friend was vague about what he wanted. 'Let the story work on you,' he said.

I made some notes, looked up some stuff on sharks, tried an atmospheric *Jaws*-type piece, then, as the deadline approached, gave up. I could see journalism in there; poetry, though, was beyond me.

Then, the day before the deadline, I wrote five long stanzas. I'm embarrassed by them now but, at the same time, forensically interested in what I wrote. Three lines in the middle scratch around the outline of a buried fear like an archaeologist's trowel:

> a malignant shift of gravel
> a rolling weight of wheels
> sucks her into some terrible awareness.

Perhaps the shark swam in at the same time as my readiness to put something on paper.

Certainly, up to that moment, I'd never written a word about being shot, not even privately in my diary.

—

In every pocket diary I've owned I write cryptic messages to myself that ghost the chronology of what was real and happening on any given day. The simple code – a set of changing symbols, words and rhetorical questions – broadens and deepens the dental appointments, monthly bleedings, chemistry assignments and bill-paying life of a twentieth-century woman.

Flicking through decades of these tiny booklets I see emotional dust sparkle on the mechanical procession of my days and I'm grateful that I did more with my life than keep appointments.

At one time I used chemical symbols to award a day its rating. Au for gold, Ag for silver, Pb for lead, Xe for the rare radioactive flashes. In graphic mode I drew (and still draw) downward spiralling arrows for moods that don't lighten; smiley faces for cat-and-cream days, and, at a time when the experience was new and noteworthy, starbursts for sex.

When I learnt a foreign language I grew bolder and began muttering to my diary in Dutch. *Godverdomme. Gek. Ongeloofelijk.* These curses have no context beyond chronology. Who or what I was damning to hell, or calling crazy or unbelievable, is part of the code and belongs to that time, that feeling. In these old diaries, the worries have vanished. Their traces linger only as echoes around the commands like *dentist 10.30* and *ring hair salon*.

The oldest survivor of the pocket diaries has a red plastic cover that is brittle and chipped, and from which the once gold numerals 1968 are almost obliterated. In a year that saw the assassinations of both Robert Kennedy and Martin Luther King, the invasion of Czechoslovakia and the Paris peace talks on the Vietnam War, my concerns are embarrassingly egocentric.

From January to April there is one downward spiral near the name *Bill*, an emphatic ENOUGH on a day in March, what look like tear drops raining on *Lake Conjola* (our family's annual holiday camp) and a smiley face near an exam result. At the start of April there are two telephone numbers decorated by squiggles and arrows; the mathematical additions of someone learning to budget; the name *Val* followed by four exclamation marks and a sad face, then, abruptly, the recording stops on the last day of the month. The last entry is a single word question, *Margot?*

Like the jolt of a mirrored reflection to someone stumbling in the dark, Margot lurches at me from across a gap of thirty-three years. Of all the notations in this and most of the other early diaries, Margot is the only word I have any memory of writing. I can reconstruct the physicality of uncapping my biro, steadying the diary on my lap as the train rocked, biting the plastic button that holds in the ink tube, staring into the blackness through a grimy window. The question is largely redundant now. Perhaps I found out that my friend caught a cold and spent the evening in bed, or that her car broke down. There is no advantage in knowing her whereabouts, nor any causal connection to be drawn between Margot missing class and my being shot.

The diary entry is a simple forensic artefact, like a bus ticket found at a crime scene.

THERE EXISTS IN MY FAMILY a sort of template for what to do with the unthinkable, the worst thing, the end game. You boil up with anger and grief for a short time, you keep it 'in house' as much as possible, and then you move on, head held high, only looking back if challenged beyond your limits.

At eighteen I modelled my survival on the example set by my mother. One of eight children, she claims to have lived her childhood in a deficit of parental love. I know that her mother, a policeman's daughter, was not demonstrative, that her rules were rigid and contradictory, and that her father was distant and censorious, but real information is scant. My mother did not dwell on details.

The rare visits from this forbidding couple during my childhood sent my mother into paroxysms of cleaning blinds and straightening our hems, and hiding all traces of the fact that she smoked the odd cigarette with my father when he came in from work. If the grandparents were late arriving and my mother became more nervous than usual, she'd smoke a cigarette then shake talcum powder on the palm of her hand and blow it all over the house.

But being the object of Victorian attitudes to parenting wasn't the only wound my mother carried.

Her much loved younger brother had been killed in horrible circumstances in 1946. A commuter train had struck the vehicle he was a passenger in one late April afternoon when he was on his way home. A local newspaper gave this laconic description of the tragedy:

> The train driver blew his whistle forcibly, applied the brakes, but was unable to avoid a collision. The truck was smashed and the two occupants, the driver aged 33 years and his passenger aged 16 were killed. The Camden ambulance was quickly on the scene but both occupants were beyond human aid.

The sudden subtraction of the brother she shared her youth with and the embargo on demonstrations of grief imposed by her parents seared an acute loss onto my mother, who, at eighteen, entered a period of lonely self-recrimination. The loss became associated with a lack of vigilance, a gap in paying attention, and built itself – in the absence of absolution from a soothing adult – into a very personal (and misguided) indictment of her own capacities for faithful care.

She always kept a large framed photograph of her brother above our fireplace. I came to know his features as well as my own brothers' (and saw similarities at times, odd flashes of recognition in certain facial expressions). Over the years the lost brother kept his hand-painted colouring – the faintest blush of pink in the cheeks – the confident gaze, the movie-star hair, and remained forever young as we (his sister's children) met and passed his age and heedlessly left him behind.

What I've come to understand is that my mother finally saved herself from melancholic self-absorption by an act of will.

And so it's been for me.

Between 1968 when I was shot and January 1972, when I married, I lived at home, worked full-time, and studied at night. The passage of time was just that, three years shaped in such a way that my calamitous event lost its glow of significance. I was cued to pick up speed and move with the troupe.

In the weeks immediately after the shooting, a few curious adults came to the house to hear more details than the newspapers had given. They asked their questions of my parents, flicking me a glance now and then, looking (I used to think) for a limp or a disfiguring scar and, finding no joy in my intact person, they'd steer their questions towards speculation about the shooter. Clearly they had theories that wanted airing.

My mother would judge the tenor of the interrogation, decide if it was leading along a path that might cast me (or them, my parents) in a bad light and nip the question in the bud. She was always two or three moves ahead of the conversation anyway and I'd watch her expression, see the warning light ignite, and know for sure that the visitor was going to be offered a piece of cake or a demonstration of my mother's latest make-extra-money-at-home device, a knitting machine on which she did piece work for a clothing store. Failing that, my father would be told to show the offender his prizewinning racing pigeons.

I understood, even then, that this was the way you survived scandal and idle talk, and, ultimately, life.

—

For the remainder of 1968 I travelled to and from Wynyard each day by train and finished the year of evening school study at Ultimo. A roster of drivers waited for me on winter evenings when the sun set early, and my father met the late train twice a week. My mother's system of checking and double-checking played like a bass line under the rhythm of those days – a simple anchoring beat: to bring me home safely.

To the observer I might have seemed quite composed, reading on the train or taking bets on the telephone betting lines at the TAB; a tall, slightly aloof figure, eyes down, concentrating on something that seemed more immediate than the immediate surroundings. The truth was I was hiding what I thought was an affliction peculiar to me, a sort of mixed-bag of nervous symptoms that I might attempt to label now but which defeated my vocabulary then. I was jumpy in both enclosed and wide-open spaces, I thought every train passenger was staring at me, I needed to sit in certain seats or stand in certain alignments that I believe now were defensive positions, and, internally, I lived with the feeling that my fuse box had blown up.

Looking back I try to place myself in the times. For many, the sixties was a decade of unshackling and speaking out. I look at the black-and-white footage and see young people marching, their hair streaming, their mouths open and loud. From the page, I hear the confessional poets coming into full voice, angry and mixed-up and lucidly sad.

My sixties memory is the sight of my first hippy in the Sydney Domain. I coveted his three-quarter coat, but that's all. A glance, a desire, a moving on. While others were letting it all hang out I had my head down, trying not to step on the cracks in the footpath. I could no more cry on someone's shoulder than fly to the moon. My operating method was containment.

Then, one unmanageable morning, I walked into a chemist shop on Wynyard station. I asked the pharmacist for something for my nerves. Perhaps I said I was upset without going into details, I don't remember. Perhaps I simply stared at him with my conflicted, red-rimmed eyes. It was commuter rush hour and I was due to start work in ten minutes. He looked at my TAB uniform and said, 'Trouble at work?' 'Yes,' I answered. 'Not sleeping?' 'No,' I said truthfully. He went behind the counter and returned with a box of Relaxa-Tabs, telling me they contained an addictive ingredient and were recommended for short-term use only. Would I promise him to use them only as a last resort, and come back in a week?

I took two as soon as I got to work and waited for the miracle. An hour later I felt something. It was way short of a miracle, more a hint of reprieves ahead. At lunchtime I took another two and discovered a capacity for mellow detachment in my personality. But there were only twenty tablets in a box. I would have to be judicious, or smart. The mechanics of keeping myself supplied gave my brain something to play with on the train trip home.

Looking up the original Relaxa-Tabs formula in an old pharmacopoeia I see that each tablet contained paracetamol, aspirin and 5 mg of codeine, hardly a shot of heroin but if one took four instead of two, the ancient benefits of drinking from the opium poppy might be briefly imagined. I regularly took four, and developed strategies for buying supplies that will be recognisable to anyone who has known the trying business of becoming addicted. I would get off at Central and buy packets at pharmacies along George Street, then train hop to Town Hall and on to Wynyard on foot.

The tablets are still made today, with a changed formula, and minus the vitamin B component that gave the originals their distinctive and quite pungent smell. Along with the stale reek of train carriages, the smell of vitamin B products spirits me straight back to those slightly desperate days of holding on.

—

In 1969 I answered an advertisement for a laboratory assistant with the University of Sydney, Castle Hill annexe. If I was to break the cycle of agitation (memories, train travel, too many people) and chemical amelioration (Relaxa-Tabs, Fishers Phospherine, any over-the-counter medication with the word 'calm' on the packet), I needed to find a job that incorporated isolation. I obeyed this instinct to change because it was coming from somewhere deep and needy inside me.

I learnt to drive, and after dropping my new boyfriend off at his job, I took his car and went over the hills at the back of Toongabbie to another convict town where, tucked away on acres, there stood a strange and slightly sinister-looking building, the University Animal House, its dark outlines and smoking chimneys offset by a surreal sea of yellow wheat. At the interview I wore my best dress, my high heels and stockings, and carried my typed résumé which now included a distinction in chemistry.

The director silently read my CV then invited me to walk with him through the building, which, he said, contained no *actual* laboratory. The job description had been invented by the university personnel department, and he seemed a little tentative about describing what the work involved.

With each step my heart sank. But if this was a test I would pass it, and smiling competently I duly noted the guinea pig pens with their stinking straw, the open drains down which a sludge of urine and faecal matter trickled, and the tall, locked cages where chimpanzees and other primates screamed and grimaced. Pressing a handkerchief to my nose I continued on to the rabbit rooms where attendants leaning on brooms gave me dismissive looks then favoured me with a demonstration of the pumping power of their best breeding buck, on to the dog kennels where I was shown the post-operative results of student vets and dentists who practised on canines, through to the cane toad room, past the mice, to end up finally in the rat rooms, where my duties (should I accept the job) lay.

I gathered that at this point most of the previous applicants had fled in tears. Looking the director in the eye I said I wanted the job and he congratulated me on being only the third female to join the establishment, the first having just left to get married, the second being an English lady, Maureen, who would welcome my company.

As I was leaving I asked him about the wheat. In the distance I could see female figures in overalls and red headscarves tagging the tall stalks. He explained that the Animal House shared the land with the agricultural research unit. I would probably meet the Ag. staff in the course of time. As I drove away I thought how wonderful it would be to work in fragrant fields with the sun on your back. The smell of animals enclosed in pens under a solid roof was already clinging to my clothes, and I now knew that the steady stream of smoke coming from the chimneys was the carbonised remains of weak, injured or surplus-to-needs experimental animals.

This strange workplace with its taciturn male staff and locked doors would become my refuge from the daily chafe of strangers on trains (and, at a deeper psychological level, the sniper's bullet) for the next two years.

I was comfortable in my white coat and happy enough in my work to partially wean myself off Relaxa-Tabs. I still took one or two at night to sleep but compared to my former usage level, this was modest. To replace, or augment, the lowered sedative effect of fewer tablets, I learnt to drink Bacardi and Coke, and to keep very busy. Maureen and I bred, raised, sorted, weighed and despatched thousands of rats to the university where they met their fates at the hands of squeamish students with dissecting tools. I developed a fondness for these small mammals and used to carry one around in my lab coat pocket. When we were alone it sat on my shoulder and nuzzled my neck, and I bedded it down at 5 pm as if it were a child that feared the dark and wanted its mother to stay.

I told Maureen about being shot. She was from Liverpool in England, had grown up a stone's throw from Paul

McCartney, and spoke in sometimes impenetrable Scouse. She came from another world that was unshockable.

Shot? Oh yeah. She knew plenty of people back home who'd had worse. Her father, a merchant seaman, still Mersey-side, used to bring home stories that would curl your hair. Her tales unfolded as we sexed weanling rats, tossing the females into plastic boxes for shipment and the males into cages (and the runts into the chloroform bin). I learnt to shut up unless I had something stunning to say. Hearing me talk about Detective Hamer she dismissed all my misgivings about his handling of the case, and its impact on my finer feelings: 'You should just have told the old git to sod off.'

In keeping with my new-start policy, I enrolled in Granville Technical College (closer to home) and transferred out of the Laboratory Certificate course into four evenings a week of matriculation studies. In 1969 I completed Year 11, and in 1970 I sat for the Higher School Certificate, timing my holidays from the Animal House to coincide with the exams. I was nervous as a cat as I prowled the school hall where I had to sit each exam. As an external student I'd taken the absolute minimum of subjects, so there was no room to manoeuvre if I bombed out. I was twenty years old, I smoked twenty or more cigarettes a day, I had a two-year on–off relationship with Relaxa-Tabs, and I was convinced I didn't have a chance against the confident-looking girls in their serious school uniforms.

The fact that I worried about doing well in my exams was a side issue to my support team. I did my worrying on my own, inside with my other nervous activity, laying down patterns that are still active today, and still as inaccessible to reassurance as they were then. My results were better than I could have hoped for. I had choices, scholarships, even some acclamation, yet was unable to hold on to the feeling of happy arrival. The outermost ring of the concentric circles

I lived in, the taut enclosure of people concerned with seeing me safely from venue to venue, relaxed a little when I got engaged and chose my courses for university. They could see an important transition coming up. My mother, especially, encouraged me to calm down and enjoy each day. There was a sense that finally, after a detour, I was about to arrive home safely.

—

When I married in January 1972 the shooting was a historical curiosity. Certainly my husband, an immigrant Dutchman, had only a minor interest in the subject. Like Maureen, he'd come from another world where the benchmarks seemed to be higher, the shock factor muted by repetition. Members of his family back in Holland had hidden a Jewish couple during the war, bombs had fallen all over the tidy countryside where his neighbours farmed, and his father had had some sort of role in the Dutch underground under cover of his 100-year-old blacksmith shop.

Two months after we married I started university. The heavy workload in the Pharmacy faculty suited my temperament; I was used to making quick adjustments, doing three or four things at the same time, grappling with hard-to-fathom data. I was twenty-one and for the first time I was the senior hand, the one with more life experience, the married one. Certain things about me began to alter: the way I dressed, the amount of make-up I wore, the people I hung out with.

In Pharmacology pracs I was dissecting the descendants of the rats I'd once bred at Castle Hill, lifting the live animals by their tails and cracking their necks on the edge of the table in a manoeuvre I'd perfected at the Animal House – the quick, clean execution.

But keeping busy brings a pay-off of exhaustion. It doesn't

show in the photographs. I look happy, focused, in my skin. We managed a social life of sorts; I cooked and cleaned and studied, and filled every waking minute with activity. But I also had nightmares, weeping attacks, and an abnormal acoustic startle response. I needed pills to sleep and ongoing reassurance that I was loved.

It's not fair to either of us to put the shooting at the centre of what went wrong in the marriage. It would never have occurred to me to cite a stress disorder in my list of faults. We loved each other, but we grew apart. We tried separation, travel, redecorating, new beginnings and more travel. The unravelling took ten years.

The toll for me was a return of anxiety and insomnia. In desperation I saw my mother's family doctor, a man excited by the new drugs that research and development had brought to the world, the pharmacological group that spelled the end of barbiturates and ushered in a generation of women who came to know and love benzodiazepines. I still remember sitting in a wing chair in the lounge room of our house, opening the packet I'd just picked up from the chemist. *Valium 5 mg. Take one tablet when required for tension headache. Do not exceed three in one day*. I had a glass of water beside me, and I looked at the yellow tablets, wondering if headaches could really be cured by something in a bottle. Half an hour later I had drifted into a blissful sleep, but not before I noted, with a feeling of radiant gratefulness, the working loose of every tightly stretched knot and fibre over the entire length and breadth of my body.

IN THE PAST THIRTY YEARS I've done very little *talking* about being shot.

To tell my story I have to indulge in that most untrustworthy of verbal expressions: the monologue. In the main, most people haven't been shot. My recounting has to be given across a divide. I am the 'other' for the duration of my little talk and at the end I answer questions, and listen to reaction and opinion. Often I end up wishing I'd never opened my mouth.

Happily I'm not locked in the 'speechless terror' that war veterans fell into after World Wars I and II. If anything, I'm in 'speechless annoyance' or 'speechless frustration' with myself. Unless you're paying an analyst or a counsellor by the hour and therefore striking a deal that you will be listened to for a set time, or unless you are a gifted raconteur or epigrammatist, the rambling sentence-by-sentence unfolding of your story will almost always fail to raise your audience to rapt attention, and more importantly, to rapt engagement with your central issues. It's taken me thirty years to know what my central issues are. I have never found them in a social setting.

Some recent work done at Flinders University WA has found a part of the brain in the left frontal cortex that misfires at a critical moment of language processing when we are trying to talk about an emotionally loaded memory.

Hearing this on the radio brightens my day. It should brighten the lives of thousands who suffer inside their stress-induced syndromes. Step by step, science is mapping some very deep mysteries. The neurological landscape of ongoing suffering is being coaxed out of hiding. Rejoice, I say, but also be aware that information will never be enough to satisfy the emptiness at the end of the disconnected line. We need the storytellers to step in at this point, the gifted narrators with poetic sensitivity and philosophical sang-froid. We need help in making sense of science's discoveries; we need information that's been massaged by the wisdom of thinkers.

—

The most frequently mentioned brain-part in stress disorders is the amygdala, a clumsy name for a strange organelle shaped like a pair of tonsils sitting in the valley between the two hemispheres of the cerebellum. Apparently if you cut open the lobes, the interior resembles coral. The amygdala lies in the limbic system, or mammalian brain, which in evolutionary terms means one stage up from the reptile brain (which is mechanical but unconscious) and one stage down from our human brain which can sing and dance and formulate theories of relativity.

The amygdala deals with the raw emotional content of shock. Hooked up to the visual cortex it sees the spider, the raised knife, the rapist, the aimed gun, and in milliseconds sends urgent messages to the adrenal glands to pump out adrenaline, the vital fuel for a frightened human. Like a deep sensor, this early-warning alarm system has a duty of care to the greater bulk of the body which, by its larger and more cumbersome nature, has to be steered away from danger. Fear messages travel upwards to the cortex which puts them in a context ('that spider may bite you') and similarly the cortex sees the spider shape and sends its own warning telegram downwards ('pull your hand away').

Our amygdala is essential in a survival sense, yet it can

get us into a lot of trouble when the intricate feedback mechanisms that mediate its response malfunction in some way. True psychopaths may have damaged amygdalas, making it impossible for them to feel other people's pain, or to fear for themselves in fearful situations. Normal people who have undergone deep trauma may end up with damage in the limbic system. The amygdala holds on to and replays the feeling that accompanied the original trauma without signalling that this is remembered fear from another time. Close by is the hippocampus, a long, curved brain-part that looks like a ram's horn and has the job of learning and remembering. It is linked to the amygdala by dendrites, bits of nerves like computer wiring soldered onto each lobe, which zap the fresh 'fear–beware' messages along the line to the hippocampus where they are assessed, decoded, and temporarily stored, for as long as two or three years. The hippocampus relays its messages to the cortex, or the thinking, deducing part of our human brain that is able to make some sense of what's frightened us.

The syndrome that develops when this fear–response circuitry malfunctions is called post-traumatic stress disorder, PTSD, now recognised as an anxiety disorder and much studied since the Vietnam War. More people suffer this disease than might be yet realised. About half of any population will go through a traumatising event in their lives, and about one fifth of these individuals will proceed to PTSD (or about one tenth of the overall population). The triggers are varied, from severe life-threatening attack, to being scared by a medical misdiagnosis. The singular thing about PTSD is that to be diagnosed with it you have to have experienced a traumatic event. There is no such thing as endogenous PTSD. The phrase 'no known cause' cannot be applied to this condition.

However, not everyone exposed to trauma will develop a

lifelong disorder. Over twenty different pre-disposing factors have been identified; a combination of two or more increases the likelihood, but does not guarantee, that you will develop PTSD. Gender, genetics, a history of abuse, depression, your socio-economic status, and especially the way you perceive what is 'safe' in your world can influence how you handle the traumatic event when it happens. (I know a woman who saw her GP about a mole on her back. After a visual examination the doctor diagnosed an aggressive melanoma and told the woman to put her affairs in order. Pathology proved the GP wrong and apologies were tendered. The woman went on to develop a stress disorder from which she still suffers. She is educated, has a supportive loving family, is not neurotic or narcissistic, and had had, up to that point, good coping abilities. What rocked her foundations was being given a death sentence in the safety of her GP's office, a place she associates with immunity from danger.)

My own unvarying avoidance of guns and places where guns are likely to feature suggest to me (now) that I've used an unconscious form of avoidance to stay on course throughout my life. Somehow I've managed to walk the line without becoming emotionally numb or detached, or 'shut down'. Where this conscious control falters, however, is at night in the surrender hours before sleep. I have a vague longstanding nocturnal uneasiness (which can come on during the day too) with no discernible context, and this, I now know, is the work of the amygdala spidering away in its cave. I don't dream about being shot. I don't have flashbacks. The conjunction of night and 'letting go' in order to sleep seem (to my amateur reasoning) to open the entrance to the cave.

Interestingly, it is during normal sleep that the hippocampus does most of its housework. 'Dreams,' Rita Carter explains in *Mapping the Mind*, 'consist mainly of a rerun of things that have happened during the day, fired up to the cortex by the hippocampus.' Under our noses, but not noticed, some benign detail of a seemingly ordinary day – a look passing between father and child, a piece of music, a word, a No Entry sign – will, when hurled into the storehouse of the cortex during sleep, trip a switch that activates a replay of old sorrows.

—

Lynne Beavis is a nurse who helped save shooting victims at Port Arthur in 1996. She said, in interview, five years later, 'I'm still traumatised. I worry there's a mass murderer just waiting around the corner. When I go out I check exits, look at men with big bags. The whole thing has been a sharp two-edged sword. I'll blink and it will all be there, like a slide show.'

Compared to many, my story is tame. But its 'softness' when placed beside bigger, louder, more shattering meetings of bullet and flesh is a determination made by others, not by me. The core experience of being shot can't be judged by a score-keeper on the sidelines.

I am not an expert on being shot, I am someone who has been through the experience and is curious about what others have made of the bang and the blood. In the Australia of today there are, unfortunately, more guns than ever before, and, recently on our evening television, a sniper abroad in Washington DC picked off innocents with an assault rifle as they went about the tasks we all perform, filling the car with fuel, walking out of a shopping mall, going to school.

Storytelling, Walter Benjamin tells us in *Illuminations*, is the human ability to exchange experiences, a most necessary exchange that will be lost unless we attend to its survival. He writes: 'Was it not noticeable at the end of the war [World War I] that men returned from the battlefield grown silent –

not richer, but poorer in communicable experience?'

These silent men, practising what we now call *avoidance*, used what leverage they had to keep a lid on the stream of frightening images that came at them as daytime shows (flashbacks) and night-time screenings (nightmares). By not speaking, they indefinitely deferred the possibility of being overwhelmed once again. But what was lost?

If the greatest obstacle to getting over trauma is the inability to transform the initial assault into what it truly is – a story from the past – then may it not have been better for me, for all of us, to have spoken?

Using my new fountain pen I took a clean sheet of paper and wrote, 'While walking home one dry moonless night in 1968 I was shot in the back.' I stared at the sentence and saw half a lifetime of suppressed emotion stalking the bold forward march of the words. My heart picked up pace, my chest felt tight, my ears turned pink. Okay, I said to my quailing nervous system, it's time to get a few things straight. It's time to speak, and to hear others speak. Prepare yourself.

Part Three

HOW HURTFULL TO MANKIND THE USE OF [GUNS] IS.
Ambroise Paré, 'Workes' (*The Eleventh Booke*, 1634)

ON THE LAKE PATH ONE EVENING my friend Terry saw a familiar-looking woman coming towards him. He stopped, they spoke, and it gelled. They'd been at high school together. In the ensuing swapping of highlights of the past twenty-five years Wendy made an astonishing revelation. Her husband Wayne had been shot dead in the Chittaway murders, a 1999 case that had rocked the small coastal community and inspired a fever of comparisons with Port Arthur.

Terry had seen the story in the newspapers but hadn't made the connection with the girl he once knew at school. He was surprised, he told me, that she'd brought the subject up. He assumed something as devastating as murder would have been, well, held back. Wendy on the other hand spoke naturally, as if seeing your husband killed and nearly being killed yourself has its place in the exchange of pertinent information. She simply stated the facts, Terry told me, not dramatically, not watching for my reaction.

Just before they parted Terry thought to mention me.

'Tell her to give me a call,' Wendy said.

—

Port Arthur has become a benchmark for measuring civilian acts of gun violence in Australia. It's a bit of a stretch in magnitude to compare two deaths and two woundings in Chittaway to thirty-five dead and twenty-one wounded in Tasmania, but there are enough common elements to concede the phenomenon of 'shooting rampage'. Chittaway was another freakish tragedy, another case of a perpetrator – a man who was an otherwise tolerable social misfit – suddenly grabbing a gun and mowing down people he didn't know or hold any grudge against. In the true sense of the word *victim*, these people were duped by fate to be at a particular place at a particular time to serve the whim of an executioner.

And so on a clear blue-sky day in April 2002 I took my tape recorder and notebook to Wendy's two-storey house on a rural riverbank, wondering what to expect from a woman whose story seemed to be on another index of horror from mine.

Driving along her street looking for the house number I rehearsed a few questions. We'd had one long and one short phone conversation in which I'd established my credentials – shooting survivor and author – but I was sensibly waiting until we met before forming any opinions. I reminded myself she didn't know me and didn't have a clear idea what use I was going to put her story to. By the time she opened the door to my knock I was having doubts about the whole project of talking to survivors.

Wendy is small, lithe, attractive, and very fit. Before my arrival she'd been power-walking along the lake path, her usual five kilometres a day. I would learn, early in our talk, that among the many high-energy hobbies she shared with her 38-year-old husband – marathon running, cycling – was orienteering: the navigation of landscape using compasses and quick-thinking.

She exuded health. Her hair was still damp from her shower. She has a lively, heart-shaped face and twinkly eyes. She made coffee while I put my things on the table and talked about the weather.

Despite my offer to work up to the day in question slowly, Wendy was on the starting blocks straightaway, ready to go.

In February 1999, on an unremarkable Sunday, she and Wayne drove to the factory units they owned in the Chittaway industrial estate. It was a simple dropping-off and picking-up task which they soon finished, and if they'd got further than the short distance back to their parked car, they'd have been home again in ten minutes to spend a quiet Sunday catching up on paperwork.

But they heard a noise. The sort of unexpected sound our brains flash their warning lights for, the unmissable explosive sound of something discharging followed by a male cry of pain.

Their units and the others in this estate housed different tradespeople: welders, spray painters, machinists, motor mechanics, furniture makers. Machining accidents weren't uncommon. Neither was it uncommon for business owners, like themselves, to come in on Sundays to make up time. Wendy thought the noise sounded like a nail gun. Wayne motioned to her to stay by the car while he investigated, saying, 'One of the guys might be hurt.' In the next row of units across the way, the back door to unit 6 was open and Wayne walked inside – straight into the path of a strangely dressed man holding a lever action rifle.

From her position beside the van, lacking any direct line of sight, Wendy heard the sound – a sharp noise like 'something heavy being dropped'. Her senses went into high alert. She started towards the door. But as she cleared the side of the van she saw Wayne, lying in the grass outside unit 6.

There was a red mark on his chest and a spreading stain.

'I've been shot, get help,' he called, sounding as if he had a heavy cold. 'Run, Wendy!'

Everything slowed down. Looking around, Wendy saw a man dressed in a long coat and hat pointing a rifle directly at her.

'Wayne was on the ground and all my instincts said, preserve yourself. Where are my avenues of escape?'

This is the orienteerer speaking. She and Wayne were practised at manoeuvres.

'I ran away from the gunman and he came after me, but not quickly. He was trying to get his aim, but in a lazy sort of game-playing way. So I started to weave in and out to make his aim harder.

'He didn't chase me, that was what was so weird. I thought of the movies where people being chased duck and weave to make it harder, so that's what I did, and then I felt a shove in my shoulder. There was no great searing pain, I didn't fall over. Blood came out so I assumed I was shot. I just wanted to get away and I made it to a wall I could get behind and hide.

'He never pursued me or tried to finish me off.'

Huddled behind the wall, which faced the street and more units across the road, Wendy listened. Already her blood loss was becoming alarming, and her shoulder felt tight, as if a blood pressure cuff had been pumped up too hard. After a few minutes she heard the distinctive sound of a VW Beetle starting up and taking off at speed.

She put the pieces together in her head. The weird guy in unit 8 had a bright green Beetle. She waited until the car's sound had receded into the distance and ran back to Wayne.

'I thought, how long have I got? I was waiting to feel faint but it didn't happen. I rang for help, then I went back to my husband.'

She lay with him, listening for sirens.

—

We were both a little teary at this point and I asked Wendy if she wanted to stop.

'No,' she said. 'It's good to cry. I don't stop myself.'

But I soon turned off the tape.

'Wayne was my best friend,' she said.

She got up to make another cup of coffee and I stretched my legs, taking in the room and back garden, but mostly trying to calm myself down.

'See that light up there?' she said.

I followed her gaze to the kitchen light in her cathedral ceiling. I thought I knew what she was going to say. I have a cathedral ceiling and it's a nuisance to change light bulbs. You need a ladder, and sometimes you don't bother because it's too much trouble.

'The bulb blew. That was why we went to the factory. To return the ladder ready for Monday. Wayne picked up some paperwork while we were there ... I could just as easily have stayed at home.'

Later, when she walked me to my car, she asked, 'How long before you stop thinking about it?'

She saw me as a veteran of thirty years. She'd made three.

I felt my neck flush. My chest ached the way it does when I'm threatened or stressed. I was more churned up than I cared to talk about.

I leant against the car, hugging my folder.

I said, 'After about twelve months I stopped thinking about it, wilfully or naturally, I'm not sure, probably a bit of both. But the forgetting began to happen, and you've got to remember I didn't lose anyone the way you did. Life went on. Other things happened.'

I looked at the ground.

Then I thanked Wendy, got into my car and did some deep breathing. She handed me a file through the window. 'It's my psychological report.'

Driving home, I took a wrong turn and then another. I pulled over to get my bearings. I opened the folder and read the summary at the end:

> It is hoped that Ms O'Shea's positive attitude continues, but clinically, on the balance of probabilities, she will need to deal with the trauma at some stage during her life. Particularly as she ages and her body copes less easily with the strain of the physical and emotional demands placed upon it and she can no longer use it as a distraction. It will be at this time that she may experience severe symptoms and disabilities.

—

The killer, Robert Hill, had prior criminal convictions for possessing firearms, prohibited weapons, and for drug use. He was single, but had a number of simultaneous relationships with women, and had recently broken up with a woman with whom he'd had a child and who reported that Hill used amphetamines and alcohol to excess. During a binge, Hill had 'trashed' her property and was said to have 'poor anger management'.

The first thing I did with Wendy's court transcripts and case notes was dive into what was known of Hill, what he did, what he said, how he defended himself, what his family made of his terrible crimes. I believed she was fortunate to possess so many pieces of the puzzle and as soon as I'd got the broad sweep of Hill's profile, I briefed myself, ready for what I thought would be a revealing discussion about motive and circumstance. But I would find myself confronting a composed silence and a downward sweep of Wendy's eyes.

'I haven't read the court notes,' she said.

There is no puzzle to solve, in Wendy's view, except the bigger puzzle of why we are born in the first place, if only to struggle for a while then die. Her picture of the crime scene is as complete as she needs it to be: Hill shot Wayne, then shot her. Wayne died, she lived; Hill went to jail. The pieces are all there. She has no curiosity about Hill and no space on her emotional canvas for painting in extra detail.

But I have a strong desire to know (as far as it's possible to know) what makes a person fire a gun at another person in cold blood. The picture of Hill taking aim at Wendy, tracking her like a fleeing animal along the sight of his rifle, waiting because he has time to wait – this picture trips too many of my own switches to let it alone.

At home, I sat cross-legged on the floor with the case file, my back pressed into the wall, and read that Hill had been living (apparently illegally) in unit 8 of the factory complex, in the row opposite the O'Sheas'. Since 1991 he'd been a member of the Comanchero bike club and kept a collection of hunting knives and ornamental swords (at least twenty were found in the unit), as well as a Winchester .22 rifle and ammunition. In the judge's summing up, he wrote of the 'prisoner's continued fascination with dangerous weapons', despite the terms of a bond imposed for a previous conviction.

At the time of the murders, Hill was living in unit 8 with his latest girlfriend, a woman of twenty-one – when they were not fighting, parting, then getting back together. Hill would stay away overnight at the home of another lady, and in fact spent the night before the shooting with this other woman, leaving her house at 8 am to return to his girlfriend and promising her he was finished with the other woman and would never leave her again (a promise he had apparently also given the second woman).

Leading up to the day of the shootings, Hill had had an ongoing dispute with the next-door occupants of unit 7 who complained that he played his music too loudly. His girlfriend testified that he liked his music 'reasonably loud'. It seems that she attempted to keep the peace with these neighbours by chatting to them, then checking in with Hill with suggestions for compromise, but the dispute escalated beyond her capacities to intervene.

The twenty-first of February 1999 was a warm sunny day. Hill and his girlfriend vacuumed and polished his Volkswagen. The people from unit 7, in what seems to have been a bit of creative pay-back, turned up their music to full volume and left for the day, locking the doors behind them.

The story is easy to follow so far and is reminiscent of noise-related altercations we've all lived through, or near. What follows, however, deviates so wildly from the usual outcomes that one loses the logic and has to go back and read it again.

First, Hill seems to have pumped himself up into a state with drugs and music. He drank tequila, smoked, took at least one antidepressant tablet (Zoloft) and turned up the volume on his stereo, fixating apparently on one line of a favourite song. Then he changed his clothes. Even though it was a hot Sunday he dressed in a long-sleeved Harley Davidson t-shirt, black leather jacket, jeans, black leather lace-up boots, leg protectors, and over this he put a Driza-Bone coat, black leather gloves with no fingers, and a black woollen beanie. He filled his pockets with .22 Magnum bullets and picked up his rifle. When his worried girlfriend asked what he was doing, he answered, 'I'm playing a game.'

Then, using his heavy boots, he smashed through the common fibro wall with unit 7 and broke into the room, his rifle raised and ready to fire.

Finding the room empty he trashed everything in sight, then came back into unit 8 clearly agitated. He asked his girlfriend to pour him a drink, but before she could set the glass down he'd gone outside.

—

Turning to the next page I got my first glimpse of the

potentially overwhelming amount of testimony it would be possible to hear and read as I sought other people's shooting stories. Where do you start, where does it end? At that moment I was in a small, barely known town north of Sydney picking my way through one chamber of horrors, when all over the country I could, if I chose, take as many paths as the maze would allow, all of them leading to blood and pain and the many faces of loss. And even then, I'd still be in Australia and have the whole world, and its history, left to engage.

The sensible response to being overwhelmed is to let go of the big picture and narrow the focus. I reminded myself that I was trying to see a killer in action, and here he was, about to fire his gun.

—

Hill walked from unit 8, past the empty unit 7 (with its now-silenced radio) to the open door of unit 6. Inside, two men were making a wrought-iron sign to hang outside their new business. Bradley Watson was welding. Michael Rasic was using a grinder and had protective covering over his ears. But even with ear muffs on and his head down, Mr Rasic heard (or sensed) something out of the ordinary. He looked up to see Hill holding a rifle. Mr Watson, who had already been shot in the neck, had slumped to the ground out of sight, leaving Mr Rasic to wonder what had happened to him, until he saw Hill take careful aim. In an instinctive gesture Michael Rasic raised his left arm and covered his chest. The bullet hit his elbow and entered his chest, lodging in his lung close to the aorta. Rasic threw himself to the ground, rolled under a table and escaped through a door.

From behind a wall he looked back into unit 6 to see Hill walk up to Bradley Watson and blow his brains out. Mr Rasic, who was himself bleeding heavily, stayed in a concealed position, stunned and shocked. He didn't move until Hill drove away.

And this is the point at which Wendy and Wayne enter the story. The noise they heard was Hill executing Bradley Watson. Leaving Wendy at the car, Wayne walked to the back door of unit 6 to see if something was wrong.

In her victim impact statement, Wendy says: 'It's hard to come to terms with the fact that five minutes in a normal average day can change your life.'

—

Having fired his final bullet, the one that hit Wendy in the shoulder, Hill walked back to unit 8, told his girlfriend she'd soon be reading about him in the newspapers, jumped in his car and headed for the hills. As he left the complex he passed Michael Rasic, covered in blood, hailing a passing car to get help. Hill flashed his headlights and gave Mr Rasic a wave.

After three days of hiding out in heavy bushland, Hill surrendered to police.

Someone has clipped newspaper cuttings of the arrest and trial and given them to Wendy. I look at Hill, handcuffed, being led away from Sydney Supreme Court by police officers. His hair is close-shaved and he's wearing a purple long-sleeved shirt, but that's as close to normal as it gets. There is a crazy look in his eyes and a smile that doesn't belong. I think if you superimposed long blond hair over the number-one haircut, you could be looking at Martin Bryant before Port Arthur.

I flipped through the newspaper reports, reading randomly. Hill's daughter told the courtroom that her father was an out-of-control alcoholic. Wayne O'Shea's mother, Shirley, kept her composure during the trial by working the rosary beads her son had brought back from a trip to Rome. There was a small story about a rock band that was practising in a sound-proof music studio a few metres from unit 6, oblivious.

Then I found a paragraph that made me feel indescribably sad. Michael Rasic said in interview, 'She [Wendy] ran screaming towards the rear of the factory bays, realised she'd come to a dead end and *ran back in front of* Hill. I thought she was gone. She had to run too close to him but he misfired. I don't know what happened but it gave her enough time to get past. It gave her a chance.'

The police found a total of eight bullets, two were misfires, two were misses, and four had hit their targets. Wendy surviving a misfire? I went back over my notes. I listened to the tapes. Not a word, not a sentence. An example, I thought, of the blessings of traumatic amnesia.

I know why Wendy doesn't read the words or look at the pictures.

—

The next time I spoke to Wendy we met at the factory units. She's done the courses, got the electrical trade certificates, and stepped straight into Wayne's place on the shop floor.

The industrial estate had been carved out of bushland, two turns off the main arterial road, and despite attempts at landscaping and colourful signage there is a barren, ersatz quality that reminds me of demountable school rooms from the 1960s.

The estate is really two rows of factory units, parallel to one another, each with its own entry road which runs to a dead end. The units are painted yellow but even this sunny touch can't lift the flat grimness of what are in effect segregated workplaces for businesses that make a lot of noise. Wendy owns the last two units in her row, also numbered 7 and 8. Her row faces the back of the second row of units. Immediately I can see 8, 7 and 6 repeated, painted above the back doors across the way, and the numbers give me a discomfited feeling.

Wendy looks very different in her workspace. She wears a blue cover-all, has grease on her hands, and (though it might be the light or the proximity of large, almost looming machinery) she looks tired, washed-out and puffy-eyed. I've brought morning tea for the team, lamingtons and donuts, and Wendy and I make small talk as the men collect their food and drink and move outside, out the back (not the front, I notice), into the shade.

After coffee Wendy and I go out the front into the rising heat, to a steady background noise of grinding, tapping, hammering and something whining in the distance. And she tells me the story again, only this time I can see the building and therefore imagine the scene.

As Wendy points out the route the shooter took, a man emerges from the bay next door to us. He is a furniture restorer and is placing one of his pieces in the sun to dry. He glances our way, listening but pretending not to. No doubt he knows. Maybe he's curious – I would be – but Wendy is concentrating on her story and I am both listening to a story of past danger and scanning for present danger. I feel exposed, lit up by the blazing sun – and another thing occurs to me: we are probably the only women in these parallel rows of small businesses. There is a raw masculinity about factory units that Wendy deals with head-on. She blends in in a way I never could. As we look at the numbered doors I say something about the imprint of a tragedy staring back at us.

Wendy, however, has another view. 'It's just walls, doors and some grass,' she says. 'It's we who lay the emotion over the top of it.'

Just there, a few feet away, is the grass strip where her husband bled to death from his bullet wound. Wendy doesn't have to be reminded. Every day she returns to the scene of the crime, parks in the same place, goes home to the same house, the same cathedral ceiling, the same bed.

She looks at the spot on the grass sometimes, not in sorrow, as I had expected, though there is an edge of something like sorrow in what she feels. 'I get a tear or two in my eye, but you get used to it. It's just a spot on the grass. I think, *That's where it happened*, but now there's somebody else in the unit, and life goes on. It's just a door, it's just a spot, the difference is I know what happened there.

'What you have to understand is, I'm really glad I was there. I'm glad because I *saw* what happened to Wayne. Had I been at home I might have wondered, Did he confront the guy, did he ask for it, was there an altercation? I know Wayne was going to help somebody, I know he copped it very quickly, it was all over very quickly, there was no pain for him, and I was there to witness it. I know what I saw. In my own mind I'm happy. I was there in his last moments as much as I could be, and that's another reason I didn't go to court to hear the case, I knew what happened, and what happened was I lost my husband.'

I ask her if she's haunted by it.

'Not haunted. I don't dwell on the shooter, I dwell on my husband, and almost in a peaceful sense.'

Unlike war widows, who often got a form letter from the war office, Wendy knows exactly how her husband left this life. After the gunman drove away, she ran back to Wayne, who was twitching as a circle of blood spread across his chest, his eyes open but rolling backwards. In a state of panic Wendy, who was bleeding heavily from her own wound, pulled the keys from his pocket and ran to their unit, opened up and dialled 000. In one of those bizarre twists that seem to accompany tragedies, the operator listened to Wendy's cries for help and asked, deadpan, 'Do you need ambulance, police or fire, madam?' to which she replied, 'I just need help.' She gave the address and returned to her husband.

In the waiting period, Wendy lay beside her now dead husband, taking one of his hands in hers, pressing her bleeding shoulder into the ground, and said a great many things to him, about love, their life together, how good and strong he was, how she wished he could be alive to see the big blue sky that was cupping the tops of the trees, about goodness and loyalty and looking after each other.

Until the police cars arrived they lay there alone.

Wendy says that, as time passes, the loss of Wayne is getting harder to bear. She now does an eight-kilometre walk with a cancer widow who is two years into her grief. They explore the phenomenon of loss in open-ended ways, not striving for conclusions or wrap-ups, just talking.

Wendy has quite extensive scarring from her surgery, and ongoing loss of sensation in parts of her hand. She doesn't remember much about hospital, but she does remember the first nights at home afterwards, the dead dark hours and the retreat of protective numbness. On one of those nights she called a help line and discovered that talking eased some of the pain. As time went on she joined a homicide victims' support group and found that, compared to many, she could keep talking when the deep emotions surged to the surface. The words to describe being shot and seeing your husband killed kept coming even if she and others around her were in tears. Listening to her voice on tape I know how safely spellbound her group must have felt. There's an element of old-fashioned gallantry in her delivery, something to do with nuances of emphasis, and staying away from sentimentality. Where others get lost between painful memories and the ability to articulate them, Wendy has traced a clear, well-signposted track.

Sitting in her office she tells me how she stays sane. Work, of course. And exercise. Before her knee packed up, she used to run hard, as if she were still in training for a marathon. 'You can't run and cry at the same time. Try it some time. You have to make a decision about where your breath is going to go.' When I (the non-athlete) stare at her, she spells it out for me: 'I'm talking about proper running and proper crying.'

She's joined a singing group and loves the way she can make her voice perform beyond its normal range. She keeps a journal, makes wish lists, goes on unusual retreats, like Buddhist cooking and minimalist camping. I'm impressed by her resourcefulness. But it isn't enough, all this busyness. Now that life has achieved a normal pattern (now that she's stopped running), the void is opening up. Fridays are bad. Weekends are a chasm negotiated on a tightrope.

—

That evening, reading Robert Fagles' translation of *The Odyssey* in bed, I came across that beautiful line, 'a blood wedding, a quick death', and thought of Wendy and her dead husband, their blood mingling on the grass, the epic (to Wendy) nature of the journey they had planned as their life's work. And I took the idea further, into blood oaths and wrist cutting, and imagined a bird's eye view of them lying in that arid man-made landscape bleeding into soil that may have taken other sacrifices in other pre-white settlement times ... and took it even further into wars in France where my grandfather's cousin died at the Somme – coming out of the reverie, as you do, with a snap back to reality.

My emotional upheaval at their story was, I realised, a measure of how much my reading of the landscape of the crime against Wendy and her husband differed from hers. And more than *how* much, a glimmer of *why*. The landscape at the factory unit tells a whole story. This is where the gunman sprang from. This is where Wayne fell, this is where

Wendy ran, this is the distance between the shooter and Wendy when she was struck, and over there is the place she called for help and there is where help arrived. The whole time we stepped out the distances and stood to check angles of vision an errant current of electricity fired strikes inside my chest and stomach, like a firecracker dropped inside a barrel beating itself to pieces.

I felt afraid.

I am a lot taller than Wendy and as she gently plotted her tale I scanned over her head, left, right, up, down.

I told her about feeling exposed out there, like a target, and how my fear-animal was now awake and pacing.

'That's the difference,' she said. 'I know the killer won't come back. He's out of the picture now.'

Even now, a day later, the fear won't lie down. My crime scene picture still has a faceless menace behind the crack of the gun. By walking in Wendy's shoes for a day I've woken up an old ghost and given it leave to walk again.

I am back in the edgy landscape of the sniper.

AT POLICE ACADEMIES trainees are drilled in straight shooting. Once trainees have graduated and moved into uniform or plain clothes jobs there is a requirement in their wage and salary package that their marksmanship be tested twice a year at a target range. They do a 'live' and a 'dry' shoot, that is, with and without bullets. Some officers train in a simulator with paint bombs.

If a policeman draws his gun he shoots to kill. All his training focuses on hitting a human-shaped target in a specific area, the 'centre of body mass' or 'kill zone', an area shaped like a tear drop starting at the hairline and ending in a curve under the heart. Under duress or threat, the officer shoots for the kill zone – not the leg, not above the offender's head.

To kill quickly and accurately, you need the best equipment. For Australian police, the firearm of choice used to be the .38 Smith & Wesson revolver, then in the 1990s (many years after their counterparts in America) they changed over to the Glock semi-automatic.

The semi-automatic can take a magazine with nine, thirteen or fifteen rounds. Once the magazine is clipped in place and cocked, the bullets are drawn into firing position with each pull of the trigger. When the magazine is empty, another one can be clipped in place very quickly. This quick loading and greater magazine capacity is the winning feature over the revolver, which takes six bullets that have to be reloaded one by one.

The business of killing (as applied to humans) makes chilling reading for the novice who comes to the topic cold. Take for instance the concept of 'stopping power', which goes to the heart of why our police have moved away from revolvers to semi-automatics loaded with hollow-point ammunition.

The revolver bullet in the traditional .38 gun was an all-lead, round-nose missile weighing about 158 grains and able to travel at a speed of about 800 feet per second. Complaints began to come in that offenders would keep running when hit by one of these bullets, and police wanted a handgun that would stop a criminal 'dead in his tracks'. Vincent Di Maio makes the point in *Gunshot Wounds* that:

> There is, of course, no such pistol cartridge and there never will be. *Stopping* an individual depends not only on the characteristics of a cartridge but also on the organ(s) injured, the severity of the wound(s) and the physiologic makeup of the person who is shot.

I found further elaboration of Di Maio's qualifications on stopping power in the findings of an American Weapons Advisory Committee convened in 1987 to evaluate semi-automatic weapons for the FBI. Eight experts (including Di Maio) tabled their findings during a three-day workshop.

To produce reliable and reproducible incapacitation, the target has to be hit in the central nervous system (preferably the brain). A direct hit to the heart, even though the heart may be totally destroyed, still leaves the target with enough oxygen in the brain 'for complete voluntary action for ten to fifteen seconds'.

To destroy an organ it has to take a direct hit, and to achieve destruction you need a bullet that will penetrate deeply enough to reach the organ.

Bigger bullets disrupt more tissue and 'hopefully cause greater bleeding'. Velocity, apparently, is not as critical as mass and design in tearing through flesh to get at the big bleeders.

Because incapacitation is hard to predict, the agent should *keep shooting* as long as the individual poses a threat. In the days of the six-bullet revolver, the agent was in trouble if he ran out of bullets. This danger was decreased by a move to the semi-automatic with its greater magazine capacity.

Finally, the experts came down in favour of hollow-nose bullets over solid lead. Vincent Di Maio, however, includes an appendix in his book, taking issue with what he calls the 'myths, false assumptions and second-hand stories' circulating about the superior destructive power of hollow-nose ammunition. Dr Di Maio is the Chief Medical Examiner of Bexar County, San Antonio, Texas, and has twenty-five years experience of gunshot wounds and forensic techniques. His eloquent chapter explains how a hollow bullet expands or 'mushrooms' as it passes into the body, crushing and shredding as it goes, not, as has been claimed, reducing the flesh to 'unidentifiable chopped meat', but certainly greatly upsetting the architecture of the intact body. As the bullet mushrooms, it slows down, and this action, says Di Maio, may in fact work *against* the objective of reaching and destroying, say, the aorta.

> If the aorta is 14 inches from the skin surface and the mushrooming bullet stops after 12 inches of penetration but the solid bullet travels for 18 inches, then the solid bullet is more lethal than the hollow-point.

Considerations like these are important to law officers, and the military, who must become expert in the business of accurate marksmanship.

In a famous Miami case, a suspected bank robber was shot by an FBI agent with a single 9 mm Parabellum Winchester Silvertip bullet. The shot went through the suspect's arm and into his lung (by which time the hollow-nose bullet had almost fully expanded and therefore exhausted its energy) but – and here is the cause for worry – the bullet 'failed to reach the heart'. The suspect then shot dead two FBI agents and wounded five others.

To the layperson, this kind of information belongs in a parallel universe where other-world rules apply. To a member of the police force or the military it can mean the difference between coming home from work, and ending up in hospital or the morgue. If the business of shooting to kill is a necessity, and there are plenty who think it is, then let it be done with as much skill and intelligence as possible, goes the argument.

And yet, mercifully, there is a powerful counter force within most of us that reels back from the act of killing.

Lieutenant Colonel Dave Grossman's book, *On Killing: The Psychological Cost of Learning to Kill in War and Society*, gave me a lot of information about this natural opposing force and somehow, sneakily, crept up on my attitudes to men with guns and allowed me to see what I'd refused to see before: the human spirit at work inside a uniform.

When I was a student at Sydney University we met the work of B.F. Skinner and 'operant conditioning techniques' (which are forever linked to rats pushing levers in my mind), but in Grossman's book I met them again as they have been applied to soldiers in foxholes.

Before the application of this technique, back in the days of World Wars I and II, soldiers who had been trained to fire at targets that looked like targets and not human beings would suddenly – in a real war situation – find themselves facing a human shape remarkably like their own. At this confrontation, the soldiers often froze, unable to fire. Grossman quotes some extraordinary statistics, with firing rates as low as 15 per cent.

Now 'operant conditioning' has come into the training picture. The modern soldier fires at a human-shaped target (sometimes the target is so human-like it spurts blood when punctured) and when he makes a direct hit he's given praise or a reward, like a three-day pass. Aim, shoot, kill, be rewarded. Keep practising and it becomes automatic. Simulate until the natural aversion mechanism in the brain is bypassed. When the real enemy pops his head up, blow it off and score the points.

Killers like Martin Bryant and Robert Hill had no need to attend sensation-numbing training to shoot innocent people. Bryant, who had a personality disorder that rendered him incapable of empathising with pain, appeared casual as he opened fire with his military-style firearms, shooting some victims at point blank range, others from as close as a metre. Robert Hill, a former member of a bikie gang known to practise dehumanising rituals, fuelled his non-specific rage with a cocktail of alcohol and drugs, dressed up like a bushranger and shot his victims in a slow-motion parody of Sunday afternoon target practice.

The long-term consequences of reflexive killing have been well known since Vietnam. Thirty years on, many veterans are still caught in never-ending cycles of guilt and psychological trauma. But modern training seeks, we are led to believe, to immunise the combatant against future self-recrimination and emotional mutiny. Many, like myself, find those claims to be optimistic, if not morally reprehensible.

—

In my thinking and reading about the act of killing people I have tried, unsuccessfully, to talk to a practitioner. I wrote a letter to a former SAS officer, hoping to get at least a glimpse into the special training these men undergo and, in that glimpse, to find perhaps a sentence or even a phrase about what it feels like on the other side of the gun. I didn't even get to first base. In my letter I stressed that my intention was to narrow my focus in so tight that the context disappeared. Now I realise how naive that intention must have sounded. The only legitimate context a soldier has for aiming a gun at another human is the context of war.

My next batch of letters went out to a list of possible contacts in the NSW penal system. I requested access to certain prisoners convicted of gun crimes. This line of enquiry is ongoing – I still haven't made a dent in the red tape. One layer of this tape concerns the issue of prisoners profiting from books about their lives and crimes, but as I wasn't offering money or intending to use names, the point seemed moot to me. Perhaps I watch too much television. I thought there might be a man languishing in a cell somewhere, a bloke forgotten by society who might like to break the monotony of his days by talking to an outsider.

My other options were gangsters at large (too frightening), war veterans and police officers. Through a work colleague I discovered a detective attached to the Firearms Unit. We made phone contact. He was involved in a special operation in another state, he would have to clear my questions with his superior, I would have to wait until he had time, he might have to call it off without notice – I agreed to all the ifs and buts and pressed the pause button. I could wait. Meanwhile, I kept searching for a war veteran. And, first, there was the intriguing prospect of interviewing someone who was free (within legal limits) to talk about her work on the other side of a gun.

While not intending to equate the shooting of animals with the shooting of humans, I am nonetheless conscious of certain parallels – the most obvious to me being that in both cases a life is taken by a gun.

There is reason to think that the ability to carry out an

act of execution is arrived at through a series of stages, a progression from some reluctant or neutral starting point, past the middle ground and through to a state of willing preparedness. This progression was on my mind when I set off on a trip with friends on another April day in 2002.

I drove south and slightly west, skirting around the bulge of Sydney's middle-aged girth, down the new freeway towards a southern tablelands town, a trip that takes several hours with stops, and passes through the Belangalo State Forest where serial killer Ivan Milat stabbed and shot seven backpackers.

North of Goulburn my guide pointed to a turning that would lead us over dirt roads, in and out of gulleys, through bush scenery that under other circumstances I might have paused in front of, on to the home of a woman I had an appointment to interview, a passionate animal lover who routinely had to shoot the creatures she loves.

JEAN IS AN OFFICER of the RSPCA. She is fifty-something, has short fair hair, a face that can switch from impish to stern in nothing flat, a deep soft voice with a London accent, and an air of authority tempered with social obligation that takes the pressure off an interviewer who has only a vague idea of what she will ask.

Officers of the RSPCA are special police constables, with similar training to their blue-uniformed counterparts. Jean is proficient in firearms, car pull-overs, high speed driving and even abseiling, which she's had to do just once to get to a stranded beast.

I was invited into her large living room and offered a choice of hot or cold drinks, or something stronger if I felt the need. It had taken quite a while to get to this house, which sits in a commanding position in the foothills and is miles from anywhere. The roads are bumpy and occasionally treacherous and I'd been wondering what it was like when the creeks were running.

My guide was Jean's daughter, Sam, who grew up in these surroundings and clearly experiences a wave of nostalgia for the wide open spaces whenever she comes home. (I know this homecoming feeling; it's gripped me many times, taking hold like a huge squeezing hug. For me it lasts about thirty seconds, then I want to leave again. On the return trip Sam would tell me how as a teenager she couldn't wait to escape to Sydney.)

While the family were reacquainting, I wandered to the

balcony to take in the sweep of the valley and be freshly reminded of how unlike anywhere else in the world the Australian countryside is. The shades of green alone do it for me. Khaki, lime, verdigris, patches of emerald where there's water.

Horses grazed in the close paddocks; kangaroos further out. Just as I began to feel the onset of a few alpha waves, an explosion of dogs was unleashed from a doorway further along the porch. These are Jean's babies, the house pack that had been temporarily penned until the visitor had crossed the threshold and taken a breath. The largest is a ridgeback cross called Rocky, the smallest are a pair of fox terriers called Rug and Rat, and in between are two border collie kelpie crosses, the newest additions (rescued from neglect). I put my hand down in a get-to-know-me gesture and after inspecting the newcomer the pack rushed off to greet Sam's young children, who had travelled down with us and would stay on for a few days' holiday when we left.

Over lunch I saw the dogs in their preferred modes, draped over settees, or sleeping close to the wood-burning fire. It had been pleasantly mild when I left home but here, in the tablelands, I'd added layers and pulled on woollen socks. After our meal, Sam took the children and two of the dogs for a bush ramble, and Jean and I settled into comfortable chairs.

I turned on my tape recorder, did a sound check, settled my notepad and opened my mouth, just as Jean's phone rang. She was not officially on duty but animal welfare, like child welfare, is not a clock-watcher's job. Of course I eavesdropped on the side of the conversation I could hear, which was Jean explaining, more than once, how to get to a farm. She returned to her chair, cradling the cordless phone that she warned would probably ring again because the caller, a female metropolitan officer on secondment, couldn't find her way to an outlying property. Jean calls her city counterparts 'metros' and takes a country person's delight in their deficiencies in recognising where property boundaries change.

'Tell me how you moved from being a rescuer of injured wildlife to an officer who has to routinely kill injured or neglected animals, specifically with a gun.'

Jean prefers the word *euthanase*.

'It's a mouthful but it paints a more accurate picture.'

One of her biggest fears when she was starting out was graduating to shooting a horse.

'They're such intelligent animals. I had it in my mind that a horse would know what I was going to do. But having shot many horses now I can honestly say they have no idea. None.'

To get to the level of competency required for horses, Jean's training began in Sydney's biggest animal shelter, the RSPCA centre at Yagoona.

Every Christmas and school holiday time the unwanted pets are signed in and temporarily housed. Those that don't find new owners are destroyed.

'I don't have a problem with putting down an injured animal, but to put down a healthy happy dog that's licking your ear while you're putting a needle in its leg, I get furious.'

De-sensitisation to putting down animals – both sick and healthy – develops relatively quickly during the training period. The transition, as Jean sees it, is not from caring to not-caring, it's more like, 'If this terrible thing has to be done, then let's do it as humanely as possible.'

'On the very rare occasion a dog didn't want to come into the euthanasing room you'd know it was a timid dog, not socialised to people, and we'd sedate it first so it was nice and relaxed.

'When you've got officers who are experienced in euthanasing and they're no longer having that massive adrenaline flow of emotion about putting in a lethal dose, the animal doesn't interpret that anything unusual is going to happen. They're perfectly calm.'

By way of teasing out the complexities inherent in animal euthanasia, Jean told me a story about Daisy, the dog out of all the dogs that won't fade into anonymity for her. She arrived at the shelter one day with a note. Her owners, a young couple, had split up. The note said how much they loved the dog and hoped she would find a new home.

When Daisy passed through the system unclaimed and was slated for euthanasia, Jean reacted emotionally to the sight of the young dog in line for a needle. It was a moment of hesitation that marked a turning point in her transition from amateur to professional. Her personal feelings had to come second to the welfare of the animal. She drew up the lethal dose, put Daisy to sleep, then moved on to the next dog.

In an aside she said (not hiding the quick tears), 'I would have done it differently today. Now I can pull strings. I'd have found her a home. Funny that, of the hundreds of animals she's the one that sticks.'

While Jean peeled some vegetables for the evening's roast, I lay on the carpet near the fire doing yoga stretches. The fox terriers used me like a trampoline.

'The first animal I shot was a sheep and I can remember standing over it holding it between my legs with a gun to the back of its head, and I found it so hard to pull that trigger. When I did and the animal collapsed in a heap I felt this incredible relief come over me. I'd hit the spot, it was as dead as a dodo. I'd been so concerned about doing it properly – I wanted to kill it instantly and not cause any suffering.'

Jean has a standard .38 Smith & Wesson pistol. 'I won't change it,' she says emphatically. 'I've had the opportunity to change but you get confidence with a particular weapon. I'm quite fond of my .38, it would feel unlucky to change now.'

Back at the beginning stages of her training, Jean was 'petrified' of guns. At the firing range she flinched at every bang and suffered extreme bouts of nervous nausea.

'When I put the gun in my hand I felt sick. The sound of it, the feel of it, even the look of it. Every instinct in me made me want to walk away.' This is a long way away from being 'fond' of your gun and shows how practice, good results and repetition can transform a receptive individual from a quivering novice to a crack shot. Jean can even laugh about her .38.

'When I'm on the job I keep it in this make-up purse, in a secret zippered pocket. It's in there with my tampons, my comb, my lipstick and a couple of strips of beef jerky that I keep for winning over aggressive dogs. You won't find too many make-up purses like that.'

Her other preferred firearm is a .22 rifle with 'hollow special' bullets. Jean has learnt to appreciate the greater destructive power of the hollow to the solid. 'Solids are inclined to go straight through the brain. I shot a cow once at point blank range with a solid bullet and it just stood there looking at me.' Having to fire a second time removed her confidence in solid bullets and set a standard for all further personal ammunition supplies.

All of her shots are head shots. She is aiming for the brain. 'You imagine a cross between the ear and the eye, diagonally there's a spot that's just right. When you're starting out it's almost tempting to carry a marker pen, but it's not a good look.'

Jean has laid out her display of killing instruments in the space between us in her lounge room. She keeps them in a locked cabinet in another room, and she has not invited me to follow her and see where the guns are kept. Her husband knows; her children and particularly her young grandchildren do not. My own unconquerable uneasiness in the presence of guns begins to work on me as she shows me the .308, her special occasion gun. When I voice my fears she counters with the standard spruik from gun training all over the world – 'A gun is a harmless piece of metal until you load it' – and demonstrates the gun safety drill of 'bullet, barrel and bolt separate'.

Jean's training has granted her the great boon of being able to move out of the red emotional zone into a green light area where drills and protocols reign. 'The .308 is so powerful you have to be careful what areas you use it in. If the bullet keeps travelling, it travels a long way. It's really meant for distance work, but one time we had a number of cattle to destroy at point blank range and the .38s and the .22s weren't dropping the cattle, they were big horned beasts, and we only had solid bullets that were going straight through so we had to revert to the .308, and I mean apart from busting your eardrums it does a very serious job.

'We keep the .308 for work at about a hundred metres range. For example, in bushfires in remote areas where we can't reach the burnt animal, or an animal falls down a cliff ledge and there's no way to climb down. The .308 really kicks your shoulder out. I have to rest it on something to take the weight. Just a fraction of an inch of movement at the end of the barrel can blow your shot.'

Suddenly the phone rang and the fox terrier on Jean's lap let out a volley of yelps. It was the metro again and she still couldn't find the farm. Jean put the metro on hold while she called in a favour from a local who would go to the officer's rescue. The issue here is animal welfare, not point-scoring. Jean worked as a metro for six months at the start of her training and knows the frustration of working from a map in unfamiliar territory. While this was going on I leafed through the RSPCA magazine near Jean's computer. I reeled back at a colour photograph of a cat, crucified on a cross. Further in there was an article on Jean and a special operation she'd been involved in, but I was drawn back to the sickening sight of the cat, tortured and dead. The magazine has only recently begun including graphic examples of man's cruelty to animals and they've copped quite a lot of flak. 'The public,' said Jean, settling back into her chair and accepting the bounding attentions of both foxies, 'can't handle it.' A quiet minute opened out and Jean got up again and turned on her computer. 'Everything we do is logged in a notebook, but I file quite a few photographs on here.' I leant over and looked at the first screen. Starved dogs on short chains. Skeletal donkeys. It was more than I could bear.

We moved to the kitchen and I got busy chopping onions. Jean told me about a recent case that had happened in northern NSW, outside her jurisdiction. There are only twenty-two RSPCA inspectors for the whole of NSW (over 800,000 square kilometres) and stories about what happens up north, or anywhere else for that matter, get passed around when paths cross, or between sessions when inspectors attend in-service courses like a recent one on psychopaths. We detoured down the psychopath path for a minute as Jean outlined the scenarios she might expect to meet one day, somewhere, when a nutter asks if he can put his own animal down (a not infrequent request on farms where guns are to hand), comes out with the firearm and points it at her instead of the ailing beast.

In Jean's experience of entering properties for the purpose of investigating alleged animal abuse, she's most often met with amazement, not anger and defensiveness, at the need for her intervention. 'People can't see the cruelty they're committing.' At the soft end of this spectrum is the man who bashed his dog almost to death for chewing the tarpaulin over his boat. The dog was kept in a clean cement and mown-grass back yard. 'I had to give the man the most basic lesson in dog ownership. Dogs need stimulation, they're part of a pack. Think "dog", don't think "me". Give the dog something to live for, a companion, a toy, some marrow bones from the butcher. Put some mustard around the tarp.' The man was cautioned and the dog taken to the vet for treatment. This is simple ignorance that may begin and end in the back yard of someone who likes to keep things neat.

At the hard end are the people who take pleasure from inflicting pain, and use animals to practise their technique.

'Who'd be an animal?' said Jean.

A large part of Jean's work is prosecutory. Under the *Prevention of Cruelty to Animals Act*, Jean has the powers of a special constable. She can enter properties, investigate what's been reported (cruel humans rarely turn themselves in), set out a report in her notebook (the same books police use – books that are signed in and out, and archived in Sydney), take statements and photographs, seize animals and items pertinent to the abuse, and work all this together into a brief which a solicitor will later present in court.

The case she'd heard about from her northern colleagues was particularly controversial and concerned interest groups she thought might have a bearing on my study of modern gun culture. It came to the department's attention because a video had been handed in anonymously to an inspector. It was the animal equivalent of a snuff movie, home-made, unedited, and indescribably vile. The action involved several young men, their pig dogs, a vehicle, a pig hunt and the sordid consequences of out-of-control behaviour, knives, staple guns and being in the middle of nowhere with no one to object. After the pigs had been brought down, the men encouraged the dogs (and participated themselves) in mutilating the pigs in a blood frenzy that turned the stomachs of the most seasoned officers.

'The attitude is, pigs are feral, but it's an offence in this country to pit one animal against another – the dogs are supposed to find the pigs and be called off. What we saw on this video was pure blood lust, the men worse than the dogs because they should have known better.'

The wild pig case was still being prosecuted. No outcome was known at the time of our talk. Jean briefly returned to the story later to make a connection that others have made, the one that shows, almost without deviation, that people who go on to commit horrible crimes (Martin Bryant is a case in point) have a history, and often prior convictions, for cruelty to animals.

And in a macabre coda to the ending of the film (a particularly awful disembowelling scene) the video flipped into a suburban lounge room where a young wife was holding a child who was being encouraged to wave at daddy, the cameraman.

This same daddy had made his pig video over the top of a home movie.

'That was his undoing,' said Jean, handing me a fresh cup of coffee. 'Somebody always recognises you.'

—

The feral pig story made me twitchy at a deep, personal level. A buried circuit in the part of my brain that holds the fear of that night in 1968 suddenly lit up and fired off warning signals. I might have been standing in the kitchen of a lovely country house but in a parallel universe I was being 'hunted' on a dark lonely road.

Putting my cup down I told Jean the story. The tape was still running so I can listen to myself all these months later and check my vital signs. Obviously, then as now, I was still wrestling with the 'magnitude' issue of the shooting, a doubt that I was carrying around like a worry bead. I seemed to massage it at every opportunity.

'When I said I'd been shot with a .22,' I hear myself say, 'there was a shift in their [the gun experts] reaction to me, as if I hadn't been shot with a real gun. Can you react to that statement?' Apart from sounding like a junior reporter, I recognise the genuine appeal I was making for the question to be taken seriously.

Jean motioned me back to the lounge chair. 'The .22 can do just as much damage as a .38, if not more. *In the right spot*. The .22 is an all-purpose rifle. If it can drop a bull, and it can, it can easily drop you. It's the preferred weapon. I shot a 600-kilo animal last week with one .22 bullet.'

I sipped my coffee so that my quivering bottom lip had an anchor.

'Guys look at a .22 and think it's no challenge. It's not a case of how much damage it can do, it's more a case of if it doesn't have a hell of a recoil and nearly knock you off your feet then it's not a gun, it's a pop-pop.' She gave me a kind smile. 'I don't think any of them would stand in front of a .22, believe me.'

Jean was almost shot herself once, on her own eighty-hectare property. She'd been down at the creek and as she climbed up the rise she felt a whistle go past her head, then the delayed sound of the rifle fire. Two men were shooting at kangaroos and had seen the movement. 'I remember thinking I'd have never known what hit me.'

—

We moved outside to catch some sun. I photographed her guns, wondering why I was doing it. The prints are still sitting in their Kodak packet unexamined now. Perhaps it's because my own brain instantly erases gun imprints. I don't want to see them and my grey matter obliges by pushing the delete button.

'Jean,' I asked, 'if you fired a .22 into the body of a sheep or cow, what would happen?'

'Not a lot,' she said. 'They'd hardly notice probably. An animal doesn't make the connection, *oh, that was a bullet and I know what damage it's going to do*. An animal can only relate to what's happening in the moment. If you've hit an organ and it starts to bleed internally the animal would eventually fall over. As it got weaker and the pain kicked in, it might start to panic. That's obviously something we never want to see. That's why we go for the brain with the first shot.'

'What if the target was a human being?'

'I can't imagine what it feels like to have a bullet go into your back. For some reason I imagine a red-hot searing pain. What I do know is, the realisation somehow makes it hurt more. With guns we've all got this inbuilt phobia that guns kill, and somebody only shoots you with the intent of killing you, as far as I can see. It's a definite act. I imagine that would add to the stress and suffering. Even if you recovered from it, you'd still be able to feel the bullet going in and hear that sound. It can't be a good feeling for you. You need answers.'

In the near distance we heard the sound of Jean's grandchildren returning, loud and happy on a king-size dose of fresh air and bush-bashing. I wished I'd been along for the trip. Jean put the firearms away. As she zipped up the last bag, she wondered aloud, 'Was it a dare?'

COMING AS I DO from a position of wilful ignorance about gun culture, I made a necessary decision to tackle some theory, to ground my anecdotal reportage.

Reading theory is not a new challenge to me so I was surprised, even a bit worried, when I ran up against a strong physical resistance to the task.

I would begin, for instance, on 'Aspects of the Priapic Theory of Gun Ownership', a potentially fascinating read in *The Gun Culture and Its Enemies*, edited by William R. Tonso, get past the intro as far as the author's treatment of Freud's tenth lecture on phallic dream symbolism, strain to keep my reasoning brain in step with the argument, take a deep breath over sentences like 'This symbolic relation [that weapons and tools stand for what is male] is the residue of an ancient verbal identity' – and on the exhale, close the book. At a guess, I think my desire to comprehend was being swamped by old, old stuff from the primitive recesses. I experienced a tight chest, butterflies, and a strong desire to watch *I Love Lucy* re-runs on TV.

Another day I took a second look. A Detroit psychologist had studied gun homicides and found that small handguns predominated over large calibre, long-barrelled firearms. He'd argued that if guns are penis substitutes, then tough Detroit crims were inviting unfavourable comparisons, and as this patently wasn't the case, the priapic theory wouldn't hold. But then the Detroit study gets the heave-ho: felons, the book argues, are not representative of gun owners; the study ought to look at hunters – as, of course, it does.

> If barrel length and calibre were priapic-theory influenced, we would only see big game rifles in the hunting catalogues. Even American hunters who could afford to specially order the .577 or .600 would not appear with them on a bear hunt because to do so would inspire derision, not respect.

So the author roundly condemns the proponents of the priapic theory, ultimately agreeing with the Detroit study, and singling out Emanuel Tanay, author of *Neurotic Attachment to Guns*, with this slap on the wrist:

> To the extent that Freudian theory is at all relevant, it might imply that it is Tanay's own 'distaste for guns' and 'reluctance to touch them' which is neurotic and/or immature.

I closed the book again and picked up the TV guide.

—

Each side of the gun debate engages in labelling and name-calling. It goes with the territory of strongly held views. What I will call 'my' side – though I'm not aligned in any official way – was characterised in one pro-gun book as upper middle class, university educated, urban living, change-oriented, internationalist, and left-wing. We own no guns, don't have friends who own guns, and consider people who own them to be 'deviant'. Compared to other descriptions I've seen, this one seems to be strenuously polite. During a reluctant visit to a gun fair last year I came across a grey-faced loony who sold T-shirts proclaiming *Death to all Bleeding Heart, Greenie, Pinko, Paedophile, Yuppie Scum*. His merchandise, which featured swastika flags and bumper stickers reading *Speak English or Die*, functioned as a set of props for his frequent theatrical rants at customers and browsers on the subject of why everyone should be armed, to wit: that 'these people' (foreigners, wogs) came to Australia for one reason only – to rape our women.

I didn't need to go to the books to find out what we called the pro-gun side. Rednecks, cowboys, men with small penises, warmongers, conservatives, hillbillies; the pejoratives, I'm chastened to say, still roll off my tongue with ease.

I once called my brother, who'd moved to the country and developed a swagger, a 'redneck' at a family wedding. We'd both had a bit to drink and I'd been listening to his cowboy tales with growing alarm. What the hell was he playing at? In the ensuing verbal stoush we let fly with a healthy exchange of name calling. Several guests standing in earshot found somewhere else to be. It was my first conscious glimpse, I now think, of the lifestyle commitment that underpins rural gun-owning.

As his sister I could hear the arguments; what I couldn't bear to hear (and see) was the posturing. No X-ray scanner or metal detector has the penetrative power of sibling scrutiny; no stone statue is less forgiving of humbug. I think it was my father who broke it up. At a signal from the groom the DJ turned up the music and before long I was dancing to John Mellencamp's 'Cherry Bomb'. From my position on the edge I watched my brother and his wife near the centre of the dancers, eyes closed, word perfect on the lyrics, grooving to old moves.

I've never been able to listen to 'Cherry Bomb' since then without filling up with tears. They were only months away from splitting up forever. They had three kids, they were 'young' and 'improving', and nobody, least of all me, was laughing when they took centre stage, pretend microphones to their mouths, and belted out the last chorus, looking straight into each other's eyes on '*yeah, yeah, yeah*'.

What I'm struggling towards is a glimpse of what it is we lose when we clamp ourselves immovably to a position; whether it's pro- or anti- or firmly in the middle, we lose a sense of the other person as a human being. The posturing, the humbug, the labelling: they're the barricades we hide our fragile and hurting hearts behind.

—

You wouldn't have got me anywhere near shooters once upon a time. My working assumption was that possession of a firearm included the distinct possibility of that weapon being fired. I had not, at that time, seen the telling phrase, 'a presumption of innocent intent', coined I believe by the National Rifle Association of America. If the gun owner has passed the character investigation and been issued with a permit, then 'evaluation of his or her *reason for going armed* [my italics] is not considered to be the business of the state'. The notion of innocent intent when you are packing a piece seemed illogical to my way of thinking about guns; and in fact, I took the opposite view, that there could be no innocence (if I understand the meaning of the word) inherent in being in possession of an instrument capable of blowing someone's brains out.

A recurring pro-gun argument reads along the lines of 'people who fear guns know nothing about them', and indeed, there is merit in educating ourselves as well as we can. I ploughed on with my reading, still agitated, but determined to get through at least one sequence of books. My notes came out like slogans.

People, not guns, are the problem.
Guns are not penis substitutes.
Guns save more lives than they end.
Guns are working tools for hunters.
Guns are sporting equipment for target shooters.

Guns are objets d'art *for collectors.*
Guns get a lot of bad press.
Hollywood and TV distort the public perception of guns.

I wrote down the stats from one study of violence on the screen. Sixty-four per cent of all major characters and thirty per cent of all characters (major and minor) were involved in violence on the screen (as perpetrators or victims). In the real world the figure is less than one per cent. I was impressed by that.

—

William R. Tonso's book gives a memoir of his life as a gun enthusiast who learnt the craft at his father's knee and could barely wait until he was old enough to go off on his own expeditions with his .22 rifle and a handgun, plinking at cans in a disused mine quarry, and taking the odd pot shot at a snake or a bird (something he now regrets). His bucolic memoir contains echoes of stories my own father tells of being taken on rabbit hunting trips by a reclusive male relative of his mother's: the mood of Tonso's reminiscence contains the same esteem for a competent senior male, the same eager curiosity about gun handling, the same preparedness to serve as a novice in the expectation of one day being the man with the gun yourself – except in my father's Depression-era Australia there was no sentimentality attached to killing rabbits, and no wasting of bullets on tin cans. Where the stories diverge, and where I begin to feel nervous about the argument being posited for private gun ownership is contained in this paragraph.

> Whether with my parents or by myself, walking out beyond the edge of town almost always meant taking a gun along. For the most part, this was done to take advantage of plinking opportunities … But there was also an underlying concern with

> self-protection, since drunks could be encountered along the tracks occasionally, and there was always the possibility that they could be troublesome.

Troublesome drunks needing guns pointed at them? This is the line I can't cross.

—

In Australia we don't have a Constitution that grants us the right to bear arms. What we have are gun laws and amnesties and black markets and the cross-pollination of other cultures where a gun culture is entrenched. The proliferation of guns in private hands is unavoidably changing the social landscape. Between 2000 and 2001, NSW, for instance, saw an increase of thirty-four per cent in the offence category 'robbery with a firearm', compared to say 'no significant trend' in malicious damage to property or robbery without a weapon.

Another phenomenon, firing guns into public airspace as a mark of celebration, is a practice most of us have only seen on television news coverage from countries under military dictatorship, yet it has arrived here.

On New Year's Eve in Sydney 2001 a family stood watching the fireworks in Sydney's southwest, when their nine-year-old daughter was struck in the arm. 'Bleeding profusely', she was taken to hospital where she was treated for what was believed to be damage caused by a spent skyrocket found on the footpath. However the pain didn't go away and an X-ray showed a 9 mm bullet lodged in her right arm. Police believe the bullet had been fired into the air and had pierced the girl's arm on its descent to the ground. In a nearby suburb a woman woke the morning after New Year's to find a 9 mm bullet lying on her lounge-room floor, and in a similar way investigations showed that the bullet had been fired into the air, had pierced the roof of her house and come to rest on her floor on its way to the ground.

Falling bullets have become so common elsewhere in the world that a scientist has calculated a table of terminal velocities, based on the bullet coming back to earth in both a base-forward and tumbling approach. His calculations show that except for the .22 short calibre bullet and the buckshot pellet, all commonly used bullets fall back to earth at a velocity in excess of that needed to perforate skin.

I WAS BORN DURING THE KOREAN WAR and had my adolescence while Vietnam was raging. It doesn't mean I know anything about war in a personal sense, merely that the *concept* as well as the *actuality* of it has always existed in my lifetime and will always loom while nations choose the belligerent alternative. My uncle by marriage was in Changi; my father and his brother were in Japan in the Occupation Forces; my father-in-law was in New Guinea in 1944. I watched World War II movies. In history at high school I wrote essays on the Kokoda Trail. I had an abstract sense that war was loud and dangerous; that not all men were heroes; that a lot of men suffered under less-than-adequate leadership and a lot died; that the survivors came home and as a rule did not discuss battle.

Of battle fatigue and war neuroses, I had the merest of encounters. Two young men I knew went to Vietnam. One married my best friend just before he was shipped out. The other was a guy I met through my first husband. Both were broken by the experience, both suffer long-term stress disorders, and only one is still married to the wife who waited at home during his term of duty.

Everything I knew about soldiers told me that they had an advantage over civilians in matters of aggression and defence. Where we react instinctively, often inappropriately, to sudden attack, soldiers have been rehearsing for this very moment during all the countless hours of their specialised training. They know guns so well they can load and fire in the dark. They know what damage a gun can do, and will probably never forget the rules and drills their firearms trainers put them through. They know how to charge on command and dive for cover. At first in simulated warfare, then later in the real thing, they've heard guns fired, seen targets and humans fall over, perhaps helped evacuate a wounded comrade.

What happens, I wondered, when a soldier is shot? Does his training grant him a magic shield that somehow accepts the shock and pain as part of the personal cost of high-risk endeavour, while preserving the ethic that got him to war in the first place?

The soldiers with the highest firing rates during actual warfare (over ninety per cent) are the men who went to Vietnam. Correspondingly, these same soldiers had the highest rate of severe, long-standing combat trauma.

I had made contact with the Australian Vietnam Veterans Association to ask for help in finding veterans who'd been shot, who might be willing to talk with me about their experience of taking a bullet. It took some writing and telephoning, and not surprisingly some 'checking out' of my credentials.

The clinching bid in my request to speak to Vietnam soldiers was that I'd been shot too. These men are leery of trivial or prurient intrusions into their memories. Being shot is not a club that invites members, but quasi-membership strips away a whole lot of preamble when you get down to the business of saying what the experience was like for you. Certain preliminaries can be dispensed with, certain assumptions taken as read.

Now this long path led me, first, to a man named Billy, a New Zealander ex-soldier living in Western Australia, with whom I've exchanged telephone calls, faxes and some ordinary old-fashioned letters.

Billy went to Vietnam in May 1969. He was one of two scouts regularly working ahead of his company like a forward set of ears and eyes, looking for signs of enemy presence. In October, eight days before he was due for R & R leave in Tokyo, he copped a bullet that would take him out of the war altogether.

If I wanted to compare the magnitude of a shooting event with my own, or others I've looked at, Billy's would have to rate high on every scale of measurement. He was shot with an AK-47, a high-velocity automatic machine gun used extensively by the Viet Cong. The impact force lifted him off the ground, spun him around and landed him on his back, severing the subclavian artery close to the top of the left lung and causing blood to spurt out in pulsing arcs. When he 'came to' (seconds of time, he thinks, less than a minute) he thought he'd trodden on a mine. His shoulder, which lay at a 'twisted' angle, hurt like hell for a brief time then progressed quickly through a dull ache to localised numbness. In a reflexive action, he called to his patrol commander, 'Hit from the right,' a signal that unleashed a raging gun battle – 'enormous firepower, five to eight thousand rounds per minute, you couldn't hear yourself think' – over his prone body. He took hold of his left arm and gave it a pull to see if it was still part of his body and finding himself intact, waited for help. Shielded by the other scout, the patrol commander crawled across the clearing and dragged Billy to safety inside the protective lines of his company. Using water from a canteen, the officer rinsed Billy's sweat rag and stuffed the fabric into the gaping exit hole left by the bullet, then called for medical aid on the portable radio transmitter.

Above the screen of support fire from both mortar and artillery, a Casevac helicopter manoeuvred into position. The heavy fire, the chopper vibration and the men's shouts bore down on Billy and the officer like the leading edge of a tornado. The chopper continued to hover – looking for, and not finding, a place to land in the thick vegetation. The canopy was too thick, the risks too great. After a second sweep the crew lowered a harness, and hands reached up to catch and secure the swinging seat that would haul Billy upwards. 'It felt as flimsy as a bicycle tyre, I was holding on for grim death.'

His patrol 'poured on the fire power to keep the enemy down, give them something to do' as the chopper gained altitude, but the return fire was so strong the chopper had to take off, trailing Billy like bait on a fishing line, skimming the tree tops, screaming his lungs out.

When they were clear of the battle, the medics winched him inside and gave him a shot of morphine for the 90-minute flight to Vung Tau, the nearest military hospital.

It took nine months of medical treatment in a northern Malaysian hospital to do what could be done for Billy's shoulder. After an operation to clean up the wounds and repair shattered nerves and bones, he was immobilised in a body cast, until infection set in and more operations followed, culminating in a scapula fusion. Basically, the arm doesn't work any more. The muscle has withered, the fingers don't move, there's no rotation. He rejected amputation (one strongly recommended option) and worked with physiotherapists in what proved to be a futile attempt to reanimate the wasted limb.

Billy has a soft voice with only barely discernible Kiwi inflections. He is a Maori from a family of military men stretching back to 1847. The photograph he sent me shows regular, handsome features and the horizon stare of someone who has seen more than most of us would care to in one lifetime. He trained for two years in guerrilla jungle warfare at military camps in New Zealand, and remembers the first time his section commander gave the order 'load your weapons' on Vietnamese soil. 'The next time we fired our weapons it would be at another human being and not at a target. I got my first taste of real fear.'

The legacy of Billy's war, apart from his wasted arm, has been what I suggested to him might be called 'manageable trauma', if that phrase comes anywhere near the mark. I was keen to know how he managed, given the magnitude of his own wounding, and the death and woundings he witnessed in his five months at war.

Going over the story again and again, listening to his voice on the tape, I came to my own amateur conclusion that two things, perhaps three, were key signifiers – history, support, and temperament. His father and grandfather and great-grandfather had been military men. The family home contained military memorabilia. There was a family language for war, and for peacetime after war where re-integration into civilian life had to be accomplished. He had the examples of forebears to model himself on. After Vietnam, Billy returned to the army and served for twenty-three years, retiring in 1991. In one sense, he didn't re-enter civilian life. He took a desk job in the army, mixed with army people, talked (if he talked) about Vietnam with army people.

He credits the huge community support he got from his home town for the absence (in him) of a sense of futility about his personal war experience. He had gone away, he'd done his job, he'd come home wounded, and his people had applauded. The telegram he sent from Malaysia with its short, unsentimental message, 'No cause to worry,' rings in Australian and New Zealand ears like a time-delayed echo from Gallipoli.

These are the big things, the safety net of concern and approval and welcome, the big three that Billy landed in when he finally made it back home.

When I took Billy back to the time immediately after he

was shot, he told me about a smaller, possibly more precious, miracle that happened. A short Maori prayer spoken by his patrol commander. 'We were still in the line of fire,' Billy wrote, 'and his [the patrol commander's] priority was to get us under cover, so this prayer was an acknowledgement of the Trinity – the Father, Son and the Holy Spirit – in our language. While he said this prayer he blessed me with water, water from his own canteen. In our culture, if we are sick or injured, our elders bless us with water. You are most welcome to quote the words:

I Runga I Te Ingoa
O Te Matua
Te Tama
Mete Wairua Tapu.
Amine.

'If time and predicament was in our favour there would have been a lot more words spoken, but these words and the water blessing gave me great comfort and reassurance. I knew although I was seriously injured that I was going to be alright. It gave me the strength I needed to help myself.'

Addressing my own themes I asked him about the *feeling* of being shot. He replied with what was becoming a familiar response: the dull thud, the confusion about what actually happened (was I shot? did I stand on a mine?); the shock of seeing blood; the numbness; the gradual resumption of sensation (meaning pain); the wondering (like Wendy) if he was about to die (is this what the beginning of death feels like?).

On bad days Billy has flashbacks. Loud noises make him cringe. Now and then he feels a wave of anxiety that starts in the pit of his stomach and travels to his shoulder. His eyes water, his mouth dries up, he loses his bearings. His mind replays scenes, frame by frame, of the things he witnessed and the men who were killed. At other times he faces the unimaginable, that his life could have ended in a foreign land when he was twenty.

'I could have come home as a telegram' is the way he puts it.

It's presumptuous of me to say I know how he feels. I understand 'manageable trauma'. I recognise a warrior spirit, with its respect for the traditions and emblems of warfare. Billy in all his communication with me has only ever used the term *Viet Cong* or *the enemy*, never the derogatory *gook* or *slope*. He speaks of his time in Vietnam as a 'job' and expresses regret that he wasn't able to complete the work he'd trained for so hard and long. At twenty he was primed to a state of readiness to do the thing well.

—

After transcribing Billy's story I dreamt about his rescue for weeks. The drab jungle greens and browns gave way to vivid technicolor, hues straight out of Disney cartoons. Perspective shifted upwards, up above the lime-green treetops where Billy was being carried to safety in the enormous beak of a giant, smiling toucan.

On the phone I told Billy a story about the time I was part of a welcome-home group at Garden Island, as eager as anyone there that day to see a man I'll call Tony disembark after his tour of Vietnam. It was about 1971 and we'd taken a picnic lunch and some beer to celebrate. Tony's wife, and the two-year-old son who was born while he was away, were beside themselves with nerves and anticipation. My fiancé and I hung back to give them room.

When Tony finally came off the ship and joined us, it was clear that something was very wrong. His expression, so dark and wounded (though he was physically sound), left our sunny smiles bobbing in the air like balloons at a funeral.

Tony had always been a brooding sort of guy who could be won over by good company and high spirits. Now he exhibited an altered behaviour that persisted beyond the homecoming disappointment. Over time, certain antisocial tics (like sitting on tombstones and carrying firearms) began to bring him to the notice of people beyond the family unit. He seemed happiest prowling in bushland, going further and further out as if trying to get lost. It became confusing for his friends to reconcile the picture of the family man (they had two more children after the war and built a beautiful home) with stories of his increasingly reckless flaunting of society's rules.

Then one day we heard he'd been arrested – but by then, most of the people who used to care (including me) had drifted, or been pushed, away.

'We never really know where people are hurting,' said Billy. 'I have a sad story too. The circumstances are different but it amounts to the same thing – pain that won't go away. About four years after I came back from Vietnam my mate killed himself. He'd been badly hurt by a booby trap over there. He was terribly disfigured, lost an arm. He was very knocked about emotionally but he always kept it together. Like me, he stayed in the army; then one day, he got up from the mess, drove to the top of the hill where we'd done a lot of our training and gassed himself inside his car.'

Good mental health depends on so many things. Neither Billy nor I can say exactly what those variables are.

—

My second Vietnam vet was Mal, a handsome, well-presented man who lives with his wife in one of the new enclosed estates that are a feature of prosperous suburban living in new millennium Sydney. His house sits on a rise at the midpoint of an oval road, tall, white, columned and imposing. I had waited some months to meet Mal. He is retired and is often away, and on this trip he'd been up north visiting a friend from the war, a reclusive guy who prefers steamy air and wet trees to the tidiness of lawns and sprinklers.

Mal's wife, Marie, spotted me circling the street and waved me into their driveway. She'd made scones with jam and cream, and served great coffee. I watched her working with freshly ground powder and thought, This woman has to be Dutch, or at least northern European. During my five years in Holland I'd been re-educated about coffee. The lessons have stuck.

As Mal painted the picture of his deployment to Vietnam, I thought that of all the dates he could have landed and begun his active service, early May 1968 had to be the worst kind of bad luck for a twenty year old who joined up in a larrikin spirit, hoping for adventures in a foreign country, a bit of 'yahooing around', and the benefits of tax-free money.

The dates made me tingle. Our 'events', as wildly different as they were, happened thirteen days apart in 1968. The Battle of Coral at Nui Dat is a well-documented encounter between opposing forces that precedes by only a few days the My Lai civilian massacre. While I was convalescing from a single suburban sniper wound, Mal was lying in an earth pit in a jungle clearing, bleeding from six places.

Trained in jungle warfare at a camp in Queensland, Mal was part of the 12 Field Regiment, a unit called the '9-mile snipers'.

'The infantry, the foot sloggers, were up front practically shaking hands with the Cong, doing the whole bit, while the artillery was behind the lines giving support. The last thing on our mind was any fear or worry of getting *too* involved.'

I recalled reading about the effect of distance from the enemy on a soldier's willingness to shoot and kill in *On Killing*:

> there has never been any difficulty in getting artillerymen, bomber crews or naval personnel to kill … all [are] protected by the same powerful combination of group absolution, mechanical distance, and … physical distance.

On the morning of 12 May his unit moved out of Nui Dat to set up Fire Support Base Coral, with Mal (a regimental police officer) among the last to arrive in the afternoon. His job was to dig a pit, an eight-by-twelve underground room to house the command post, then, when that was in place, to dig his own machine-gun pit. It was tough physical work, and by the evening meal-time they were eighteen inches into the ideal depth of six feet for the machine-gun pit. It rained, 'it poured', they ate their meal, their weapon pit filled up with water and Mal and his colleague, a bombardier, chatted about the heavy work waiting for them next morning. Around midnight, a burst of machine-gun fire and green tracer suddenly erupted through their position and the whole atmosphere of routine and getting ready for some future engagement, if any, immediately soured. The men got into their weapon pits and waited. From his forward position Mal saw movement, which he reported by radio to the command post. He was told, 'It's the mortar platoon, don't worry about that.'

An hour or so later, 'all hell broke loose' when they came under rocket and mortar fire. Mal discovered later that the regiment had set up position practically on top of Viet Cong troops who were waiting to advance on Saigon. These 'nogs', as he calls them, had been watching the Australians set up and dig in, waiting to choose a moment to strike with maximum effect under cover of dark.

Between Mal's weapon pit and the Viet Cong were the mortar soldiers, ten of whom were killed during the first wave of the attack. The Australians were able to fire off splintex shells (canisters containing thousands of small lethal darts) from three of their big guns, disabling large numbers of enemy. However, in their shallow pit, with no contact and no line of sight, Mal and the bombardier could only guess what was happening all round them. They lay on their backs – 'it felt like we were in a coffin' – with no cover, just the night air above them and the booming sounds of a battle. They could hear shouts for medics, shots going off, and nightmare sounds of men groaning in pain. They fixed bayonets. From the command post the sergeant called out an order to fire the M79 grenade launcher. Mal had three grenades and got two away before losing the third in the dark. Their machine gun jammed after one round of firing, so the bombardier, the senior of the two men, shouted, 'Fall back into line,' meaning retreat to the command post, and led the way with his rifle at the ready. Mal stood up and made to follow when he was hit.

'Next thing I was on the ground, then I realised I'd been shot. It knocked the rifle out of my hand and I looked to see what'd happened. It was dark, I still had my raincoat on, I couldn't tell. My stomach felt crook and my wrist was hanging off, the shell broke the bone and exploded out the back, and I'm laying there, thinking, they say the nogs cut your throat, so I got myself back to the command post, I don't know how. And the blokes thought I was the Cong. I yelled out "Gunner Hundt," and he called back, "Roll down the side," and as he grabbed me his rifle went off and he shot me in the back of the leg. "Sorry," he says.

'That wound didn't hurt, but I do remember the warm feeling of blood running down my calf.

'I was under cover now, I lay there from 2 am to 6 am. My wrist was going numb so that was bearable, but my stomach, I really knew about that.'

During his four-hour wait in the command pit Mal received the minimum of medical attention. Someone applied a shell dressing, but in the absence of a medic, and the more pressing business of defending themselves against attack, Gunner Hundt was left to his own fate, and the hope that his fit young body would last until dawn.

Outside, a tremendous battle was being fought. The Viet Cong temporarily overran one of the field battery's gun pits; American gunships arrived to help; the ammo bay caught fire.

It was dawn before they could put Mal on a stretcher and transport him to a place where a helicopter could land. Like Billy's rescue, the operation did not go smoothly. Just as he was about to be lifted a sniper shot twanged past their heads and the bearers dropped Mal on the ground. He was dropped twice before finally being hauled on board and flown to the US 24 Evac Hospital.

During the flight he received a medic's attention, some pain relief and reassurance, and, he remembers wryly, the best he could do in return was vomit on the wounded guy below him.

At the hospital he learnt to his surprise that he'd been hit six times. Once each in the bladder, bowel, wrist and back of his leg, and twice in his foot (ankle and heel). He woke up three days later looking like a patchwork quilt of stitches, connected to intravenous fluids and an alarming number of drainage tubes, a catheter, and, to his horror, a colostomy bag. 'I was cut everywhere, I looked like Frankenstein.'

The next two weeks were a blur of surgeries (six on his shattered wrist), infections, pain, and the growing fear that he was finished. When he was awake he watched the parade of wounded, the amputees, the guys missing half their heads, the mutilations that seemed beyond any human attempts at repair. He rejected the attentions of the ward priest (fearing, he told me, that he was about to be given the last rites).

During his training, Mal, like his fellow soldiers, had

undergone anti-enemy indoctrination. They'd trained in mock villages where they learnt that innocent looking villagers could be Viet Cong in disguise. He learnt not to be fooled by 'black pyjamas' or innocent faces. He learnt about booby traps, holes in the ground with spikes, and throat slitting and torture practices that had left indelible prints on his psyche. Rationally, today, he has a changed attitude to war and deplores the waste of young lives, but he cannot rewrite the old messages concerning the Vietnamese enemy.

In the US hospital, towards the end of his stay, he noticed that one of the beds was taken by a wounded Vietnamese woman. The idea that she would sneak up on him in the middle of the night tortured his mind. He stayed awake watching her.

After two weeks he also was flown to Malaysia for treatment (and in another blow to his suffering body, was dropped off the stretcher again during a transfer), and finally home, to two Australian hospitals. At Ingleburn he had more wrist operations, and at Concord he had his bowel repaired by a new technique which saved him a lifetime of wearing 'a bag'.

Like Billy, Mal stayed on in the army until he retired. To some extent, the bad treatment of Vietnam veterans by an uncomprehending general public was cushioned for him by the companionship of soldiers, among whom he had the status of having survived wounding in one of the big battles of the Vietnam War.

—

As our interview wound down I asked Mal what it felt like to be shot.

'The first sensation was being knocked off my feet, like I was hit by a baseball bat. It was blunt at first. Nothing happened for a while, my fingers went numb where the wrist was hit. As for the ankle and heel shots, I never felt them at all, ever. I didn't know about being hit there until I was in the hospital. It was the machine-gun hits to the stomach that worried me the most, I can't explain the feeling. It was a dull rotten cramp, like something was *really* wrong.'

In 1993 when Mal was being assessed for medical classification, he had some X-rays taken as a matter of routine. To his amazement he discovered he still had two bullets in his abdomen. This information had never been given to him abroad or at home, during all the medical treatment he received in four different hospitals under the attentions of field and civilian surgeons and medical staff.

'Why on earth not?' I asked.

'They're 9 mm bullets,' he said, shaking his head slightly.

I'd been studying ballistics on the run in my preparation to speak to shooting survivors, but the significance of his answer went right over my head.

'The nogs didn't have 9 mms,' he said. The sentence hung in the air.

After a little pause, I asked him about flashbacks and bad dreams. His wife, Marie, who'd sat quietly through the interview, watching Mal's face and keeping her hand inches from his, answered for him, 'Yes.'

His bad dreams can be triggered by something he's seen (TV, news), and often by smells (wet earth in particular). Frequently the dreams seem to come out of nowhere for no reason. Marie wakes him up.

'He might go for six months without one, then have two in one month.'

If he visits an army buddy, as he'd done recently, daytime emotions and night-time dreams surge, peak, then wane.

'I try not to cry,' Mal says, 'even if I feel like it.'

As I was leaving I asked Marie about her background. She and Mal were engaged before he went to Vietnam.

There is a steadfast, rock-solid quality about her. She is Mal's biggest safety net.

'You're not by any chance of Dutch descent?' I asked.

'Yes,' she said, looking surprised.

—

My guess, based on purely circumstantial evidence, happened to hit the mark. It speaks of the unconscious noticing that goes on when we are immersed in a new environment where everything from the leaves on the trees to the way we prepare coffee is different. We don't necessarily mentally photograph the shapes of the leaves; we register their otherness, and we adjust.

I had been thinking, before I located these two ex-soldiers, that their experiences would be of another order to civilian woundings, and, in many respects, that was the case. Bigger guns, bigger wounds, choppers hovering over the jungle canopy, raging battles. The scenes are familiar to us from film and television. They are scenes from another zone where mad kings rule and decisions are made on the run.

But when we strip away the florid spectacle and the deafening soundtrack, what we find on the ground is a man with a wound. His shoulder, or stomach, hurts; his own warm blood leaks into his boots; he is excused, for the time being, from participating in duties. The bullet, like a stage manager's hook, has dragged him off the stage and, for him, the war may be over. The entire event can take as little as thirty minutes. The big picture melts away, and he, like the service station attendant back home who was shot for the evening's takings, is a man alone with his pain.

—

Turning the pages of *Life* magazine I found a black-and-white photograph of a beautiful young girl jammed into the corner of a car seat by a strange looking man who was holding a gun to her throat. The girl was Silke Bischoff and she had eyes like a frightened gazelle. Quickly I moved on, willing the image to fade, then I turned back because it wouldn't. Please tell me she didn't die, I thought, looking at her symmetrical features, her stylish blonde hair, the wide spacing of her eyes that suggested the young Deborah Harry.

Turning to the notes at the back I read the photographer Rolf Nafziger's comments.

> Two bank robbers took this very pretty girl, Silke Bischoff, who was 18 and her girlfriend hostage. My Bonn office called and said they were in Cologne. I went downtown and found a big crowd – reporters, cameramen, onlookers – standing around the car in a shopping area. I had found a position at the car window when one robber put his pistol to the girl's chin. Then the car pulled away. Later I heard that the police had shot one robber (the one in the picture) and that the girl had been killed by the other robber. I do not feel good about this picture. That pretty girl was very brave. I never thought she would be killed.

The unfolding hostage drama, I later read, had been watched by twelve million TV viewers in August 1988. Silke (from Bremen, Germany) endured fifty-four hours of this cruel limelight before being executed. There are other pictures around, some on the internet. I found a colour image. She's not in the car this time, she's standing. A gun is pressed under her chin, her eyes are closed. The gunman looks pleased with himself.

Eddie Adams' famous photograph 'Street Execution of a Viet Cong Prisoner', from 1968, stands alone as a prototype of confronting record-keeping in dangerous times. Revisiting the image, I still feel the same flinch (a shocked recoil experienced by a whole generation who mounted global anti-war efforts on the backs of images like this) and I get drawn into the same polarities: the apparently brutal South Vietnamese general extending his arm to fire a bullet into the head of a bound, defenceless Viet Cong prisoner. Compositionally, the photograph has winning features (and, indeed, won the Pulitzer Prize). The general and his prisoner are framed in a street scene on the edge of a road that narrows into the left corner, drawing the observing eye into the scene over the outstretched arm holding the gun. On the right side we see apartments and a young man in a cap crossing the road looking in the other direction, as if oblivious to the execution taking place a few metres away. To the left of the general we see a soldier in a helmet, half out of frame, watching the execution with what might be a pleased look on his face, or might be a squint into the sun.

I read an interview with Eddie Adams in which he, like Nafziger, later regretted taking his award-winning photograph. Associated Press commissioned Adams to spend time with the general – hoping perhaps for more heart-stopping war images – but Adams soon discovered that what had appeared to be an act of spontaneous cruelty was in fact the final scene in a much longer drama. By delving, Adams got the back-story, and a closer look at his dramatis personae. The general, it transpired, was a much-revered local hero. He was in the middle of a bloody civil war and the execution was a reprisal for a series of murders that included American soldiers. The terrified victim in the checked shirt was the bad guy, the cold-blooded killer who broke the truce to shoot when the shooting was supposed to stop.

The context for the execution photograph disturbed Adams. 'The general killed the Viet Cong; I killed the general with my camera,' he wrote in *Time* magazine.

But Adams has the advantage on most of us who come to the execution photograph ignorant of context, back-story, character profiles and political complexities. The higher part of our brain that demands context and considered judgment is sidelined by the cries of protest rising from the emotionally charged back stalls.

—

The potent force of any gun-to-head image is the horrible knowledge that this is a 'before' picture. Our imaginations are left to construct the kill shot, the terrible blast that extinguishes all vital expression, including the frightened stare.

The Silke Bischoff picture won't leave my head. She is forever poised on the edge of her annihilation in the pages of *Life* magazine and I find myself worrying about her, as if it were in my power to intervene.

PERVERSELY, THE 'AFTER' CONDITION, specifically the after-medical-assistance condition, has often aroused my scientific curiosity. As macabre as it might seem, I've felt obligated to be present at some end-point of a shooting incident, in the neutral, rather archaic role of scribe.

To this end, I approached people with contacts in hospitals and morgues for permission to see the wounded living and/or the recently dead.

I know what my own healed scars look like; I've seen Wendy O'Shea's incisions; and I have shared an afternoon with Dennis, a young American man who was shot in the heart (and survived) and now wears a defibrillator sewn into his chest wall.

The next step seemed to be the *not-for-public consumption* versions, the freshly made, and *post mortem*, wounds.

Medical personnel working in cities where shootings are an everyday occurrence will be surprised to learn how difficult it is to put oneself at the shooting victim's side when (as in my case) the nearest big public hospital has seen only two shooting cases in the last five years. Given that it takes me hours to drive in to central Sydney, there hasn't yet been a confluence of timing and availability for me to go ambulance chasing (and there are the necessary barriers of permission and courtesies that take time, and reduce my chances of being there to see and hear and vicariously feel the medical commotion that attends trauma).

A writer once told me that when he was researching for

his crime novel he was lucky enough to be invited to watch an autopsy. An old school friend was a morgue technician who smoothed the writer's way to the autopsy room where he witnessed the post-mortem on an apparent suicide. The young woman appeared unmarked and nothing was immediately obvious. The experience of watching the autopsy had a sobering effect on the writer. He could not, as his trained friend could so easily do, step into clinical detachment. The girl was about the same age as his daughter. He hated the way she was laid out, naked, unknowing, and sliced open while music played and technicians chatted. He was surprised by the amount of fluids and blood, and the tangle of organs and tubing a body contains.

When they opened the girl's skull the cause of death revealed itself. She had shot herself through the roof of her mouth, and the bullet had ricocheted inside the cranium, mashing her brain to pulp.

The writer came away with more forensic detail than he'd ever hoped to know.

After listening to him, and observing the lasting effect of the experience on his psyche, I gave up the idea of pursuing the autopsy observation. Not because I'm squeamish – when I worked in hospitals I visited morgues, I've seen and smelt death from the doorway, and my capacity for behaving myself under duress hasn't yet let me down. But the post-mortem in a shooting death would be different. I realised, listening to the writer, that I couldn't be sure, then, of controlling an impulse to psychically merge with the body on the table, to identify with a possibility that it could have been me.

There are books aplenty to satisfy anyone who wants to know what a skull looks like when it's been penetrated by a bullet. The photographs are as gruesome as one would expect, and the science of gunshot wounds as complex as any specialty area of surgery.

But like any hard-core experience, seeing multiple examples of the worst can have a blunting effect. The truly rattling encounters, the images that hurl their fear missiles like well-aimed javelins, are often located in what comes before – in our human capacity to rise to a heightened state of anticipation.

—

Lisa is 38 years old. She has a round face, soft curling hair and blue eyes whose expression and inviting openness remind me of TV moms from sixties' sit-coms. She was born, educated, had her first job, married and had her two children all within a ten-kilometre radius of where she now lives. A sense of home, and belonging to an urban community where most of the faces are familiar, are two of the most noticeable indicators of what Lisa means when I ask her what 'feeling safe' signifies for her.

When she was thirty-six, before the seismic shift that cracked open her life, she used to live in a pleasant house in a street where most of the families were young and her husband, Kevin, a self-described workaholic, had recently started his own business – contract cleaning and handyman services – which Lisa supported by distributing leaflets and taking phone calls while holding on to her own job as a part-time pharmacy assistant. To the wider community they had always seemed ideally suited. They laughed at the same things (in fact they laughed a lot), they enjoyed the same leisure activities (like trivia nights at the club), they spent a lot of time with their children (Lisa is a volunteer reader at the school, Kevin coaches the football team), and when they're together they relate stories like entertainers going through a well-executed routine, each happy for the other to linger over a detail, both faces poised at the same degree of animation.

But even before her address changed it was becoming clear that since the business 'took off' and Kevin had begun spending up to fifteen hours a day doing tough physical work, the family who at first applauded his entrepreneurial energy were beginning to complain about his absences – and to dread his silent, depleted presences.

I'd known Lisa for some years: we used to work together at a pharmacy occasionally, and then regularly when I took on an alternate Sunday job to save for a holiday. Between prescriptions we coloured in selected details from our private lives, which, from Lisa's perspective, were galaxies apart. Her assumptions were predicated on the fact that I was the pharmacist (therefore better educated), had no children (therefore could afford travel) and was writing a book (therefore had more interesting friends).

I didn't contradict her utopian version of my life. It was easier somehow to relate to her from my other galaxy, to act the role of the anthropologist who knew little or nothing about how she lived.

Over a period of time I met her husband and children when they dropped by, and as the weeks rolled out like carpets ending in every other Sunday, I spent nine-hour days on the job, in her company.

So when Lisa failed to show one Sunday and I was told she was taking time off because of her 'nerves', I was surprised but not overly concerned. I presumed she'd had a showdown of some sort over Kevin's work schedule.

But there turned out to be a far more sinister reason for her absence. One evening she'd gone to the supermarket and a man had put a gun to her head.

—

My mind played with all sorts of gun-to-head images – all

the stored-away terror scenarios – but I didn't get to hear the detail because Lisa stayed away, I went overseas, and a year passed. In the interim I held on to my imagined picture of Lisa and her ordeal.

When the opportunity arose again, I asked about her. Her colleagues were keen to fill me in. Being menaced in your local food store is an event most of us dread. Lisa, the chosen one, was the lucky survivor who represented the rest of us, who (a) never believe bad things will happen to us and (b) pray that if bad things happen, we too will be spared.

The next time I asked (after a gap of months), Lisa still hadn't come back to work and her story had acquired a new, less sympathetic spin. I was told she'd agreed to work certain shifts, had turned up, taken up her position behind the counter, served one or two customers, then fled the premises in tears.

Finally I heard she'd been replaced. Her behaviour, so un-Lisa-like, had become intolerable in a commercial enterprise. Lisa, it seemed, had dwelt too long in the land of the victim. Favours and forgiveness were gradually being revoked.

The TV mom had fallen in a graceless heap.

—

Eventually Lisa and I met again and I saw noticeable changes in her appearance. Her lashes seemed permanently wet, and there was something different about her hair, it had lost its bounce and looked limp, like her mouth. We worked a day together, a Sunday during a busy summer trading period, a day when extra staff had been rostered (and Lisa had been offered another chance to prove herself). As sometimes happens in summer, things got a bit hectic. The atmosphere was tense and, I have to say, foreboding. Customers seemed to be on edge; I was on edge. Small incidents loomed large. I wondered what phase of the moon we were in, I kept looking at the clock wishing I was on the beach or in an armchair reading, instead of paying off my travel-induced credit card debt; and in the background stood Lisa, pale as a wraith, giving off adrenaline vapour trails.

'Something's going to happen,' she confided to me. 'I can feel it.'

This sort of thing is catching. I locked the back door, even though it meant blocking a flow of fresh air, then, when things quietened down, I closed the alternative entry into the store from the side street. Now, anyone who came in had to enter and exit the same way. And yet, even with precautions (or because of them), still, as if we'd conjured him up, a churned-up young man asked if he could use our private toilet as there were no public ones for miles around and he was desperate. He looked slightly mad to me. I was all for telling him no, but it was Lisa who unlocked the security padlocks and showed him the complex of corridors that led to our rather degenerate shared amenities block out the back.

The reward for her compassion was that he didn't come back. And short of scaling a cyclone fence and its barbed-wire fringe, he *had* to return the way he went in. There was nowhere he could be, except (I was convinced) slumped forward on the toilet seat where he'd shot up on pure heroin and killed himself.

But we had four hours to push through and a shop full of people wanting prescriptions and suntan lotion. I put my head down and concentrated on the job, reassuring the increasingly nervous staff that if the man was dead he wasn't going anywhere, and if he wasn't, the back door was now locked so he couldn't get at us. This worked for about thirty minutes, then Lisa rang her husband. I lifted my head at the tone of Lisa's voice and saw the terrible toll the waiting was having on her. She was seriously, clinically agitated.

By the time Kevin showed up we were uncomfortably stretched. The junior assistants had reached the limit of their capabilities, and Lisa was in a crying jag. Kevin, clutching a heavy spanner, headed for the toilet block while I directed traffic using a voice more suited to football crowd-control than friendly family chemist practice. I felt like Basil Fawlty routing the hotel guests for complaining about his manner.

Clearly, Lisa's reaction was out of all proportion to the implied threat of the vanishing man. It spoke of problems in need of attention. I could see how her employer, having accommodated her altered state for so long, had then given up in exasperation. And it was clear that Kevin, who'd had to leave a job to come to our rescue, was none too pleased that his wife was in hysterics again.

The vanishing man, it turned out, had used the toilet then got lost in the corridors, ending up at the back door of another shop where he had knocked, been grudgingly admitted and shown the front door.

At closing time I first broached the idea with Lisa of interviewing her for my book about guns and trauma. She seemed to fit the criteria of someone suffering from a protracted disorder.

—

Lisa's encounter took place on Father's Day, September 2000. She'd invited a few guests for a meal and at the last moment found she was missing a couple of ingredients. She asked Kevin to do the five-minute drive to the shops and when he cried off, claiming Father's Day privilege, she decided on what was probably the quicker option anyway, going herself.

When she got to the checkout, she put her few things on the counter and was checking her purse for change when someone screamed.

'It was an awful sort of scream – I turned to my left and

the person two feet away from me was the robber. He had a gun pointed directly at me.'

The scream had come from the checkout girl, a teenager who was now huddled against her co-worker, also a young girl, both of them trapped inside an island counter from which customers buying eight items or less were served.

When neither girl moved, the man raised his voice. He was, Lisa said, extremely jumpy, and grotesquely dressed in black.

'He had a fake black beard on, long and black, a black outfit, black tracksuit pants, black jacket, black hat. My first reaction was: this is a joke, he was so heavily disguised you would swear it was Santa Claus all in black.

'I can remember thinking, from my training in the chemist shop, my first reaction was to hide my rings. I curled my hands up like this and I kept my mobile phone up under my right hand like this, thinking this is the only thing that's going to get me any help. I let go of my wallet, I thought he can have that but I kept the phone with me. Anyway, he threw some plastic bags at the two young girls on the checkout and one of the bags dropped on the floor, but the girls, being young, they just froze, and I could see that they weren't doing what he was asking and that scared me, so I stepped in a little bit there. I kept saying to the girls, "Put the money into the bags." I said, "Come on, girls, give him what he wants."

'Anyway, one of the girls went to lean down to pick up the plastic bag that had dropped and I said, "Don't do that," because I was frightened of startling him, he might think she was going for an alarm button. I stopped her from doing that, but at the same time they weren't progressing in putting money in the bag, they were just really scared and I kept saying, "Come on, girls, just do it!"'

At this point in the story a security guard suddenly ran into the store.

'He was yelling at the top of his voice and the robber just lost it. He started screaming he was going to blow us all away. He held the gun at each of us, towards our faces, yelling abuse.

'It just went on and on, it was echoing through you in the end it was so loud, because the security guard was – anyway, the security guard was screaming too and saying, "Get out," and then I heard the click of the gun and, um, I actually heard, I counted, four clicks, I think it was four clicks of the gun, and in that instant I looked at the security guard and – sorry –'

Lisa broke down at this point. She was clearly inside a vivid live replay of the clicking gun. Her face was pale and I could almost hear her heart pounding across the table. She apologised, and I offered to suspend the interview.

The training Lisa referred to is a standard part of modern pharmacy accreditation. There are very well laid-out rules for what to say and do when a robber makes a demand. Put simply, the response is: Give the thief whatever he or she wants. Be passive, don't make sudden moves, don't threaten. In pharmacies where I've worked we've often made jokes along the lines of 'would you like your money gift wrapped, sir?' and 'would you like fries with that?' in those silly moments when the conversation idles into the imagined world of what-if-we-were-robbed.

Finding herself suddenly transported to this imagined land, Lisa strove to remember and implement the drill, only to be sabotaged by two rookies. The girls were fifteen and sixteen respectively. They'd been employed by the supermarket for a couple of months, after school, and both were competent cashiers and givers of the correct change. Neither had been to training school, both lived at home with their parents, and the worst incident each had had to face was the failure of management to put on enough staff to cope with the extra trading on Father's Day.

In her optimistic belief that applying the robbery drill and calling on her own cunning would save the day, Lisa was relying on the pre-existence of a dynamic like the one she was used to in the pharmacy. And clearly, these young girls were not going to defer to her as the trained senior staff member. From where they were standing she was a customer trying to give them orders when they were already panicked by a man with a gun.

Meanwhile the unarmed security guard picked up a shovel from a display bin and brandished it at the robber.

'There was this display, you know, for Father's Day, a whole lot of shovels in a dump bin and, um, he [the security guard], he picked one up and brought it above his head and, um, was screaming at the guy to get out, you're not getting the money, and at this stage, I really couldn't tell you why I did it, I could still hear that gun clicking and I didn't know if it was going to go off, I don't know anything about guns, all I knew was, you know, I felt I had to run for cover and I just ran.'

In her flight, Lisa came upon several staff members and customers hiding behind a stand. She quizzed the staff about the back door and, learning that it was locked, led the small band of people in another direction. One of the women began to scream and Lisa covered the woman's mouth with her hand. Directly ahead was the cool room.

'I said, "Come on, get in," so we opened the door and all of us got inside the cool room.'

They huddled in the total blackness. Lisa pressed buttons on her mobile phone until she got some light then rang 000.

The group stayed in the cool room for seventeen minutes with Lisa relaying information in a three-way interchange between herself, the phone operator and the police cars that were on the way.

'We could hear the sirens, but they kept telling us not to come out until it was safe. The police finally came to the cool-room door and said he'd gone.'

And what of the robber? The security guard had lunged at him with a shovel and the man had run away, without taking any money. I asked her about the gun.

'The police tend to think that, I dunno, the police tend to think he was an amateur and maybe he didn't have bullets for the gun, because I believe, I dunno, I believe it was a real gun by the look of it and by the sound of the clicking, it wasn't, it didn't sound like a plastic gun. They can't, no one will probably ever know –'

A note of apology enters when Lisa tries to analyse. She kept apologising all through our talk. I recognised the spectre of odious comparison, if it can be called that, undermining her testimony. Does it really matter if the gun was real? She thought it was real, the other people in the drama thought it was real, her brain thought it was real. The circumstantial evidence seems to militate against it. Why, for instance, would a man with a shovel prevail over a man with a gun? Why didn't the robber fire off a warning shot to frighten the girls into filling his plastic bag?

'It was a small pistol. They showed me pictures and we all agreed it was a small pistol.'

As a result of her inability to move beyond this experience, and the failure of three different counselling techniques supplied by agencies, Lisa has been diagnosed with post-traumatic stress disorder, and her life, her job and her marriage have all broken down. She has all day to sit and talk to me. The world outside her front door has given up on Lisa.

'I always thought I was a stronger person. I thought it would go away if I ignored it. But it hasn't. It might for a little while, then there'll be something like I'll be walking down the street and see someone who looks suspicious, or somebody in a dark jacket that reminds me, or a dark hood, or a dark beard, a really dark beard, and then all of a sudden it comes back like it was yesterday. Only last week I went into the bottle shop and went to walk into the cool room to get a cask of wine, and I couldn't do it. I went absolutely stiff and could not go into that cool room.

'I'm taking an antidepressant. At first they put me on something for sleeping, but I couldn't handle it, I felt awful. After three weeks they put me on Aropax. I can tell if I forget to take it because I don't cope as well as I should.'

FOR SOME TIME NOW I've been reading books about post-traumatic stress disorder. I write down facts in a spiral-bound notebook, think about the information and move on, like a grazing wildebeest (or your average neurotic), to the next bit of interesting-looking pasture. I am, of course, looking for descriptions that finger me.

This is a subject that's excited researchers into an almost immoderate amount of publishing. And I can see along the research's linear path an enormous shift away from scepticism into genuine, testable confirmation that such a syndrome exists, and is deserving of our attention.

My interest began selfishly. There was a time, some years ago, before I bothered to do any reading, when I used to say that victims are born, not made. My position was based unscientifically on one case, my own, in which I argued to myself that by choosing *not* to be a victim of a shooting, I had not become one. The extension of this kind of thinking is that anyone who has been through an ordeal and hasn't recovered from it is in that dark victimised place because that's where they want to be.

I remember reading a story in a women's magazine about Germaine Greer being attacked in her own home by a deranged student. The journalist must have been trying to extract a victim impact statement, because Greer's voice suddenly growls with frightening resonance off the magazine page: 'I am not the victim here.'

Whoa, I thought, I'm with you, Germaine.

—

During the 1970s and early 1980s I travelled between Europe and Australia quite a number of times on very long plane trips. From a confident beginning, my aeroplane passenger competency began to deteriorate, progressing quite rapidly into teeth clenching, wide-awake hyperawareness of engine sounds and vibration. My remedy for fear of flying was a cocktail of alcohol and benzodiazepines, and knew its worst delineation in a stopover in Bangkok where I was led zombie-like by my partner from plane to hotel and back to plane with no memory at all of ever having set foot in the city.

These days I use my frontal cortex like a stern schoolmaster when I'm in a plane. The method is not foolproof (and, scientifically, it's invalid) but I endeavour to overpower my fear by an effort of conscious will, coupled with conscious work. I give my brain something to do. Watching films and reading novels won't do it, neither will music. What I do is make lists. Not just any list, lists that require concentration and the effort of recall:

Name (or describe), in order, all the people you saw today since 10 am.

Write down every address you've ever lived at, in order of tenancy.

Every boyfriend. Possessed and unrequited. (P) and (U).

*The names of all the characters in the TV series M*A*S*H,* their rank, job description, hometown, nicknames, and real-life names.

Writers I have met, or seen from a distance, (M) and (S), since my first book was published.

Ten minutes of turbulence is a cinch, provided I have pen and paper.

Flying post-dates the shooting and I can't imagine that

they are related in any way, but strangely the dread feels the same.

Since I began revisiting the time I was shot, the dread has started following me around. Thanks to my prodding and poking, a steady stream of phantoms and ghouls have been leaking from what used to be a very well-sealed vault.

And lists don't come anywhere near zapping them.

I had a panic attack one evening when my husband was away. For a few days before, I'd been feeling dizzy and tight in the chest, and had seen my GP, who could find no somatic symptoms. When I told her about this book, my lip began to tremble in an embarrassing way. Public crying is not an activity I relish, nor is the prospect of admitting to emotional weakness, yet here I was dangerously on the verge of both activities. My doctor suggested I speak to a counsellor, and produced a business card for someone she'd heard good things about. I got out of the room as quickly as I could, and after some thought, made the appointment.

—

The disorder Lisa has been diagnosed with has gone by many names, as different societies in different times grappled with individuals who clearly have not recovered from some shock. Constant reliving of the shock eventually dissolves the glue that fixes that person in relationship to family, to neighbours, to workmates, and finally to the social fabric.

From the scientists, we know that the instant Lisa saw the gun pointed at her head, an emotional memory was being laid down in her brain. Real gun or fake gun, the body reacts in the same way: heart rate and blood pressure increase; defensive and anti-inflammatory hormones cascade into the bloodstream; nerve endings fire like Gattling guns, releasing chemicals that will find their way to vital organs carrying an urgent message, *prepare yourself for danger*. Blood is diverted away from serving the gut to serve the greater masters, the brain, the heart, the muscles of the skeleton, the frontline forces of the great cumbersome machine they in turn serve. The blood vessels in her skin draw in their girth to limit bleeding should the man strike her. As the skin vessels contract, her feet grow cold, and the chill spreads upwards to the knot in her stomach and makes the tense muscles supporting her rigid posture ache with strain. Deep inside, the body's stores of glucose are thrown overboard into the bloodstream, flooding the waterways with dissolved available fuel. Even the endorphins are put on stand-by to blunt any forthcoming pain.

Inside her brain, elaborate computations are triggered by the warning bell that rings even before we consciously know we're in danger. In milliseconds the fright/flight system is activated. Under other circumstances, Lisa would have immediately got the hell away from the man with the gun, but she was forced to stand still for too long. Hormones and neurotransmitters, the swift-footed scouts that make sure the fixed bits of anatomy link up, keep sending the same signals over and over, and the amygdala, already excited, goes into overdrive, burning an unconscious memory of the stressful event onto its hard drive. Meanwhile, the hippocampus, which creates the conscious memory of the gun, is soaked in stress hormones and instead of rendering a faithful copy of the gun event, it lays down fragments, random images instead of the whole picture.

This is a place we've all been. Joseph Le Doux, in *The Emotional Brain*, gives the example that fits Lisa's experience like a glove:

> The victim may recall precisely what the gun looked like but not be able to recall the robber's face. Later however they may find

> they have developed an aversion to beards, crooked noses, bright blue eyes – some characteristic exhibited by the tormentor but which they don't know they know.

The good reason for the release of these chemical go-betweens, the rapid construction of coping strategies in the face of danger, is permanently spoiled when the event is laid down imperfectly in our memory banks.

How and why Lisa's experience changed over time from a single ugly encounter to a state of perpetually remembering and reliving aspects of the day itself, the man, the gun, the clicks, the cool room (that is, from a 'response' to a 'disorder'), can nowadays be almost completely explained by brain mapping and psychology.

The question boils down to, why does it persist? Why can't Lisa 'get over it'?

A number of predictors have been identified by researchers, working across the range from combat trauma to natural disasters. Two of these predictors are the magnitude of the event and the amount of social support after the event.

I am very interested in the magnitude of Lisa's experience. A noticeable difference between her experience and mine is the ordering of events. With a gun pointed at her head, Lisa anticipated her life coming to an end – compounded with the big imponderables, why me, why now when I'm not ready, and even more basic fears, like, will it hurt, will I suffer? What happens when the curtain comes down? With each second of her ordeal she was tormented with a new fear.

Looking down the barrel of a gun waiting for it to go off is a vastly different experience from being shot by a sniper. There is time for imagining many different outcomes: pain, mutilation, bleeding, dying quickly or slowly, and, beyond yourself, children growing up without their mother, parents losing a daughter, a husband losing a wife.

For me, the shooting happened first, and was the last thing

I was expecting to happen. I didn't have time to fixate on the gun, its size and shape, the shooter's demeanour, colouring, age. That came later. And this sequencing seems, to me, to have a bearing on the way my memories are stored and retrieved. We know that the more dangerous (or perceived to be dangerous) the initial incident, the more charged up the amygdala becomes and the easier it is set off next time. My amygdala didn't know what hit it.

When a trauma sufferer seeks help, he or she often faces the delineating experience of a triage assessment. And this assessment, by its nature, hinges on the *magnitude* of the event. Treatment providers require shorthand language for sorting the range of personal wounds into workable categories. The expectation on the part of the sufferer is that their wounds will be accorded some respect. Unhappily, this doesn't always happen. In the book *Achilles in Vietnam*, Dr Jonathan Shay calls this phenomenon the '*pissing contests* of survivors, within and across groups, each group [claiming] that their experience is the only significant one'.

Imagine Lisa, I think to myself, trying to tell her story to a combat survivor. Imagine trying to stack up her clicking, possibly fake gun against an artillery barrage along the lines of *Saving Private Ryan* or *Band of Brothers*. Dr Shay tells us that 'Holocaust survivors have disparaged the writings of incest survivors as merely *confessional*'. People like Lisa learn to shut up, to become defensive about the details, to find refuge in cryptic allusions to some sort of 'incident'.

Jonathan Shay shows with exceptional insight the pact that is broken between a soldier and the military organisation he serves when men are put into dangerous situations for no good reason. The soldier experiences a betrayal of 'what's right'.

Soldiers joined up for all kinds of reasons – to fight for their country, maybe escape boredom or poverty, or to see foreign countries – then found themselves on the receiving end of petty revenges exacted by senior officers: extra duty, night watch, dangerous patrols, all of which were tedious or 'unfair' in a safe context, but which translated into real danger on the combat field. 'They perceived that [the] distribution of risk was unjust.'

Listening to Lisa's tape I can hear very clearly her cries about what wasn't 'right' on the day she was held up, starting with her husband's insistence that he stay at home and enjoy the privileges of Father's Day. At our first meeting she said she'd gone to the shops with 'good grace'. At the second, she expressed her anger at him for not helping when she had a houseful to cook for.

Then she let fly at the security guard.

'I was really angry with the security guard for not keeping us safe – I was more angry with him than the actual robber for a while. The guard made things so much worse and put us all in so much more danger, everything would have been much calmer if they'd just given him the money. This guy was desperate, he was shaking, willing to do anything, the way he was acting he would have lost control if he'd had bullets in the gun.'

There was anger and frustration too at the young girls who failed to comply with what Lisa considered to be the well-known strategy for saving your own skin in a hold-up, that is, handing over the cash as quickly as possible. Avoiding heroics. Avoiding inciting the thief to violent acts.

There is an issue of control in Lisa's protests. Had she been able to implement the hold-up drill she might have given the robber his money, seen him on his way, and avoided the escalation that followed. But her readiness to obey her inner control dials was sabotaged by the (to her) incompetent junior staff and the blundering, mock heroic antics of the security guard. The only time she was able to galvanise her talents was when she broke free of the stalemate and, astoundingly, bravely, rounded up her band of frightened bystanders to run for cover in the cool room. This same issue pervades the stories of Vietnam troops whose lives were compromised by incompetence and blundering.

The second predictor, the failure to find ongoing support after the first flush of interest wanes, the thing Shay calls 'communalization of trauma', looms large in Lisa's story. Her colleagues, from whom she expected loyalty, began by spreading her story in the spirit of fellowship and ended by demoting her experience to 'hysteria'. Her husband maintained a patient, sympathetic bearing for many months afterwards, but when he deemed her grace period to be overextended he joined the chorus of detractors.

'You go through a lot of different stages – anger, heaps toward the security guard, then towards the robber because he'd taken away things I'd done for years, with my husband because he didn't understand, with people around me because they didn't understand what I was feeling. I *do* try to see it from their point of view – I would probably find it hard to understand too – but I've been stripped of my safety, and I've got a lot of anger: I rebelled against Kevin – why didn't you go down to the shop instead of me? – then I get to the teary stage and feel sorry for myself, why me, that sort of thing.'

The owners of the supermarket, and the employees who were directly affected, offered cursory expressions of sympathy.

'I didn't get much support from the company at all. I was even told the girls weren't allowed to talk to me in case I took legal action.'

Having exhausted her private network of listeners, Lisa rang the number of the counselling line that had been handed to her at a short debriefing session at the supermarket. She progressed from the phone counsellor to face-to-face sessions with a government agency, and finally to the Victims Tribunal.

Having been steered in the direction of counselling myself, I asked Lisa what she got out of the experience.

'It was mostly talking, helping me to relax and sleep. And helping me as a person. I couldn't understand why I couldn't put it aside, I still can't.'

My understanding of PTSD is that talking cures are not always successful against the powerful emotional memories stored in the more primitive reaches of the brain. Emotional memories are forever, the books say. And the frontal cortex, no matter how clever at warfare, has difficulty silencing the squeals of fright emanating from the limbic brain.

So what, if anything, came out of these talking sessions?

One of the counsellors encouraged her to buy an exercise book and write a final chapter to her story. Another removed the supply of office tissues and told Lisa to 'cry it all out'.

'Why take away the tissues?' I asked.

'She said if I let the tears dry on my face I'd feel better.'

'And did you?'

'Not really,' she said. 'It just felt sort of sticky.'

Did anyone venture a theory that made any sense to her?

'They thought I had a really severe reaction because I was in such heavy control mode at the time. If I'd cracked up when the gun was pointed at me things might be easier now.'

'What would make you feel better?' I asked. In the silence that followed I added, 'For example, if all those support people who didn't support you – if they turned up now and said sorry?'

'It would help.'

Lisa and I had coffee after I turned off the tape recorder but we could barely manage the small talk that goes with sharing a hot drink. I looked around her flat, overcrowded with the furniture she'd taken from the marital home. The room, for all its attempt at the conventions, had the feeling of a bunker; the CD player which had been turned down, not off, during our interview was set on repeat, the same ten tracks over and over again – Lee Kernaghan singing about loss.

There was a sound at the front door. I turned around to see the door ajar and Kevin just outside, his key in the lock. 'He's here to pick up the children,' Lisa said, walking over to unlatch the security chain.

By the look on his face I suspect he'd also come to see what was going on. While not overtly hostile, he eyed off my tape recorder, and despite Lisa's efforts to stake a claim for privacy in her own home, he leant on the kitchen counter and asked if a working man could get a cup of coffee. Some old feminist circuitry fired up in me but I held my tongue. This was not my battle and this was not my house. I packed up my things and Lisa walked me to the door.

Did she have any last comments?

'All along I've had to defend my right to get help.'

Part Four

THEY SAY A WRITER SHOULD HAVE SOMETHING TO DO WITH HIS HANDS (BESIDES TYPING, THAT IS). PULLING CAT HAIRS FROM THE HUDSON BAY BLANKET SEEMS TO BE MY HAND THING. THAT AND SHOOTING.

William S. Burroughs, 'Last Words'

THE DAY I WENT TO THE FIRING RANGE I spent a fidgety hour deciding what to wear. Casual, sporty? Quiet, dignified? A skirt or trousers? My indecision (displaced onto my choice of clothing) marked, I believe, an attack of extreme self-consciousness about how to relate to firearms, a kind of first-date nerves syndrome, unsure of what signals my earrings and bits of twinkle might send.

Guns live, mostly, in a male domain. The gatekeepers I imagined to be gruff and blokey. In the end I chose a navy blue, long-sleeved blouse over loose Balinese pants. The top half of my attire (according to colour theorists) was screaming *keep your distance*. Guns and I had, after all, unfinished business.

The Indoor Shooting Centre west of Sydney is a blue cement-block building that resembles a large rectangular bunker, but was once, I'm told, the local skating rink. Gun etiquette begins in the carpark. The sign on the entrance door reads *All firearms are to be in cases, bags or covered before entry*.

I sat in my car watching for some minutes, intrigued by the steady comings and goings of men carrying what could be golf bags but were not. On a humid Wednesday in January, who would have thought so many people would be armed?

My scalp was already tense from map-reading and the recurrence of a miss in the engine that $600 worth of garage work was meant to have fixed. I grew up in the western suburbs of Sydney and had once worked at the Nepean Hospital, yet I'd been having trouble recognising the old landmarks. The open spaces had been colonised by medium-density housing. The vistas that had once led the eye across grassy plains to the Great Dividing Range now stopped at landlocked communities with very small yards and trees no higher than the serious-looking brick fences.

I reminded myself: I was here to fire a gun.

I sat in the car, windows down, assembling my kit: notebook, tape recorder, pen, extra pen, comb, lipstick. I'd brought a briefcase and a handbag and couldn't decide which to take inside. A handbag seemed silly in a shooting gallery. More cars arrived. The sight of men unpacking guns in a carpark made me wince.

I thought of Dante, losing 'the true way' and finding himself somewhere he'd rather not be. I could always turn around, no one was twisting my arm. But the clincher was the trouble my niece Nicole had gone to, to arrange this visit. Nicole is a secretary in the Sporting Shooters Association of Australia, an irony not lost on me. I'd kept my surprise to myself when she joined the organisation, knowing her to be a smart, talented girl with highly developed powers of discernment. She is also a tall willowy beauty. I secretly wondered if the blokes gave her a hard time.

Satisfied that I had my kit ready, I locked the car, crossed the carpark, and stepped inside the glass doors.

The first noticeable sensation, to a novice like me, was the sound of dull thuds deeper inside the building. I hovered in the entrance hall, unzipping my bag for no particular reason while trying to get my bearings. A sign directed me upstairs to the Sporting Shooters offices. Once there I scanned the cubicles and glass-doored offices until I saw the top of Nicole's head and could let out the sigh of relief I'd been holding in.

Nicole came forward in her usual way, arms extended, looking a million dollars in her short-skirted black business suit.

'Auntie Gail!'

Having no children of my own, I extract full value from my extended family, and my heart did a little maternal flip as we embraced.

She was having a busy morning, she said, and would hand me over to the relevant people then come down later to check on my progress. Okay? She gave me an appraising look. 'You'll be fine,' she added. 'Truly.'

We did a quick circuit of the offices, said hello to her colleagues, collected a mountain of pamphlets and ended up at the registration desk.

'A few preliminaries and you're on your way,' said Nicole, giving me another hug. Leaning into my ear, she said, 'I've got the best man we have to show you around. You'll be surprised.'

—

Before anyone can go near the shooting zone, there are forms to fill in.

Are you a criminal, a maniac, a grudge-bearer? Have you been convicted of an offence in the last ten years? Are you a drug addict, an alcoholic, do you have a mental disorder? Have you been the subject of an apprehended violence order?

I handed over my driver's licence and a fee of seventy-seven dollars, and was escorted downstairs into the gun zone.

The focal point of the inner sanctum was the counter and the ammunition store. Smiling red-shirted assistants bantered with members as they bought bullets. I stood near the counter, trying not to stare at anything in particular, especially not the men shooting targets, while I waited for my instructor. As soon as he appeared I understood the full import of Nicole's message, 'You'll be surprised.'

My friendly gatekeeper was Theo, and it would be hard to describe him as anything but a tall handsome man with blue eyes that looked as if they'd been polished by a jeweller.

We moved to a table where I sat while Theo got us coffee from the vending machine. I noticed the staff and members giving me the once-over, but I also saw Theo favour each of them with a back-off stare.

Sporting shooters in this country are a somewhat ghetto-ised group. People like me who hate guns find it incomprehensible that grown men come out mid-week to play with their weapons, the same weapons that can be turned on innocent people doing ordinary things. And people on my side of the fence have written powerful and damaging pieces for national newspapers about the folly of shooting for sport. I expected the shooters to be suspicious of me. I fully expected Theo to be as charming as a wife-beater in the courting stage of a reconciliation. The truth is, I could have slipped into this place of guns and bullets like a spy in disguise but I'd chosen to come in the front door because I didn't want our positions compromised by surprise or deceit.

Over coffee, Theo had a few things to point out. The first was terminology. A gun is a *firearm*. A *weapon* is any instrument used for attack or defence. A gun is always a firearm. In some cases, it *may* be a weapon.

'The distinction is important,' he said.

Fair enough. I made a note. Later I looked up the Macquarie dictionary. *Touché*, Theo. A *weapon* can be a sword, a rifle, a cannon. It can be a metaphor: *the deadly weapon of meekness*. In Zoology, it may be any part or organ serving for attack or defence, as claws, horns, teeth, stings.

During the two-hour drive to the shooting centre I'd

rehearsed a couple of ways to tell my story to the hideous macho gunslinger I'd conjured up. My preconception of the gun apologist who would take pleasure in my gauche manner around the hardware of marksmanship began to feel slightly off the mark.

Nevertheless, I had to begin somewhere, so I told him I'd been shot a long time ago, I didn't like guns, and I was here to fire a gun for reasons I wasn't quite clear about in my own mind. I left it at that and took a sip of coffee. I was aware that I was constructing a version of myself; small part shy girl, small part damaged goods, and big part intelligent not-to-be-spoken-down-to woman.

Theo, with his pale blue Northern Hemisphere eyes, seemed to have my measure before I'd taken my second sip of coffee. This was his turf, he was the man, yet he claimed no particular advantage, except familiarity with the terrain.

Instead of the expected one-syllable slow talk for hicks, I was treated to a comprehensive introduction to ballistics. To the background accompaniment of thuds and the occasional frightening detonation of a high-calibre rifle in the bunkers to our rear, Theo showed me a range of live bullets and laminated diagrams and began the naming of the parts.

'Women in general are easier to instruct,' he said when the lesson came to an end.

I was the only woman present and the generalisation annoyed me.

'In the first place, they listen.' And as if to underline his words, I noticed self-consciously that I was leaning forward, pen in hand, trying not miss a word. 'Men, I find, don't want the *spiel*, they just want to get their hands on a gun and start blasting away. They'll fill in the details for themselves later.'

A quick glance around the room confirmed me as the only note-taker.

'We do get women coming in,' he continued, 'out of

curiosity, or for a laugh – like the group who came in for someone's fortieth, and asked if they could shoot targets for a trophy. So I said, why not, and I took them through the prelims and set them up and there was this one woman who thought the whole thing was a waste of time, she wasn't into it at all, and I let her be, everybody's different. But a funny thing happened when I set up the targets and the girls started getting serious. The quiet one wanted to have a go, and she turned out to be the best shot, she had a good eye, great control, and ended up with the trophy. Now it's an annual thing. They make a day of it.'

This anecdote led him to the second part of his theory on why women are easier to instruct. Their pulse rate. Man the hunter experiences a testosterone-amped rush when he aims a gun. The extra fuel bumps up his blood pressure and breathing, and the anticipation prevents him from achieving utter stillness. Women, not quite cold-blooded cows but near enough to it in the hunting analogy, are less hindered by excitable biology.

He continued the instruction. Primer, propellant, projectile, brass cartridge cases. We looked at different shapes: straight, bottle-necked, tapered. Then I experienced information overload. Rimmed, semi-rimmed, rimless, rebated and belted cases. When we started on calibre I recognised something that's happened in my own field: the persistence of older systems of measurement alongside metric numbering, so that there are guns of .45 of an inch calibre, and guns of 9 mm calibre.

The preliminaries were protracted and handsome. Peripherally I could see men and guns in firing attitudes. Most were standing or sitting, one man was lying on his stomach and the noise from his bunker was awesome as he shot at his target. On the table in front of me were brass bullets. Behind the counter to my right were firearms and ammunition, and beyond, in an area of muted light, were display cabinets of period rifles and guns. Here we had the gun as friendly, tamed and polished exhibit; as far away socially from the wild, primitive thing that attacked me as a zoo exhibit from a hunted rat.

At some point Theo decided I was ready to enter the shooting zone. As usual I was carrying too many things, and he found me a locker.

Just as I was stowing my stuff, Nicole appeared.

'So?' she asked.

'Don't tell anyone but I think I'm starting to enjoy myself,' I answered.

'Great.' She waved at Theo, squeezed my elbow, invited me to have a sandwich with her before I left, and hurried away.

Theo had assigned us an area away from the professionals, and as he led me past the practising shooters he called out either 'visitor' or 'tourist' – my memory has them mixed up – and I fielded speculative looks as I passed by in my protective glasses and ear muffs.

During our prelim and coffee, outside the soundproof barrier, I'd been monitoring my increased heart rate, thinking, I've been in worse situations: this isn't air turbulence at 35,000 feet or the dentist's drill, this is manageable apprehension. But inside the shooting zone I was having doubts that I could carry this exercise through. My usually well-behaved sweat glands became overactive, my chest locked up, I could feel my heart trying to escape through my ears. Breathing deeply, I followed Theo to our bunker where he closed the common door and we could speak without shouting.

'We'll start with the .22 rifle,' he said, his tone neutral. To my intense embarrassment I'd developed a hand tremor which both of us were pretending not to notice.

To shoot, you have to sight, and to do that correctly

a basic benchmark has to be set. Are you left- or right-eye dominant? As someone who writes with my right hand I thought I would be a right-handed shooter, then discovered the opposite to be correct. My left eye did not want to squish shut so that my right eye could look through the sight.

In my stall, seated at a table arranged for a left-handed shooter, I was danced (it's the only verb that describes the movement) into intimate contact with a .22 bolt-action rifle – and the effect was strangely seductive.

I nestled up to the smoothly polished wooden grip, put my left eye to the sight, and let my right hand work the bolt action.

The target was fifty metres down a lane that somehow seemed like a bowling alley but wasn't, and ended in a hill of sand.

Squeeze, bang, hit. Five shots. Reload.

After twenty minutes of this I became my father's daughter – a pretty good shot, attentive, accurate, mindful.

Theo retrieved the target via a pulley line, and explained about clusters. I looked at my handiwork and surprised myself. Surely, though, I could do better?

'Take as long as you like,' said Theo.

When I stopped, I had to reset my mental gauges. Don't forget why you're here, I told myself. Ask questions. Probe. Confront. I asked Theo if he hunted. He looked as if he'd been waiting for this question. Not so much any more. Mostly culling. Kangaroos, foxes, that sort of thing.

Strangely, I couldn't work myself into a lather about foxes running for their lives at that particular moment. Arguing seemed a waste of valuable time. I could do that later, in another place, with my reference books around me.

Theo asked if I wanted an introduction to hand guns.

We moved to another stall and I was given stronger ear muffs and a talk about recoil and stance. Lock the wrists, lock the elbows, grip the gun firmly with both hands, breathe, exhale, sight, fire. We began with a .22 Ruger automatic. The sound was louder and I fought the recoil. 'Lean into it,' shouted Theo, 'let your locked arms move upwards.'

Other senses came into play. The smell of gunpowder. The way the moulded steel rests against the skin.

I had to fight my tendency to turn my whole body towards the tutor's instructing voice, complete with aimed and loaded gun. Theo stood against my left side and blocked my swing.

'Turn your head only,' he shouted into my protected ears. Twice more I swung my whole body plus gun in a wild arc. I was full of fear and seemed incapable of taking direction.

Next, he handed me a .38 Smith & Wesson revolver. A bigger gun with a bigger noise. Every Western movie flooded in. I spun the barrel, sliding the bullets into their neat little chambers. Yes, I thought, I can see the attraction.

The next gun case opened on a 9 mm Beretta, a lethal horror that peaked my anxiety. The romance of the old West took a nose dive. The Beretta evoked darkness, dirty business, quick fixes. It felt like a dense, compact apparatus for killing. As I shaped up to the target I knew that never in my life could I ever aim this thing at another human being. It felt like an unexploded bomb in my hand, and as I found my grip and raised the gun, elbows and wrists locked, the unconquerable tremor returned. What would I do if this gun were pointed at my head when I was in the supermarket minding my own business? Most of us have heard and seen handguns 'go off' in movies, we know vicariously what is about to happen, how much the air is about to be disturbed, we know there will be blood and tears.

'Have you seen the *Dirty Harry* films?' Theo asked next. He was holding a gun box of considerably more solidity than the 9 mm. The .44 Magnum is, I admit, a handsome object, heavy and large in the hand, with a long barrel and the sense of immense strength and purpose. The first were made in 1970 (so they post-date my shooting, I thought gratefully) then disappeared from the market in 1977, only to return in another era. Theo offered me the .44, but only if I felt ready to try it.

'It's loaded with target rounds,' he mentioned, a qualification that meant nothing to me, until he explained that even though the noise and recoil would be noticeably greater than with previous pistols, it would still not be as great as if I were firing 'factory rounds'.

I was dismayed by my body's unwillingness to rise to the occasion of a .44 Magnum. I'd been listening carefully to Theo's guidance and, having come so far, naturally wanted to show good faith by going that extra mile.

As I lifted the gun (it is about 300 grams heavier than the .38) I was attacked by dread. My locked wrists wavered, my heart beat faster and I lowered the gun, wanting to get it away from me yet unable even to put it on the table because of Theo's rule about setting down a loaded gun.

'Please take it away,' I said.

Theo fired off a shot for me. The sound was terrifyingly loud. Over my shoulder I saw two young men in the public area drawn by the noise. This spurred me on and, when I finally managed to steady the .44 and lock on the sight, I'd determined to fire, if only to prove myself to the audience – but even the added weight of teenage scorn couldn't tip the balance. I was incapable of pulling the trigger.

'Breathe out,' said Theo. 'Now breathe in, out again, hold still, now *pull*.'

This time I did it – to the accompaniment of an involuntary piercing scream which amused the boys and, in an odd way, released some of my pent-up pressure. I only managed to fire one more round from the .44, again with the scream, but Theo and I deemed that twice is better than never, and he fired off the rest of my clip.

My most urgent need at this point was to leave the firing booth, the claustrophobic contained area of the bunker, and breathe. I went straight to the cafeteria and sat a while with my head in my hands.

After a bit of grooming I said goodbye to Theo and joined my niece for a quick sandwich and a tour of the library. At each turn in this labyrinthine building I had an increasing sense of a powerful paternal hand resting its weight on a holstered gun; the sense that, in here at least, good sense and protocols prevail over any reckless impulses in armed citizens.

Then I slumped in my car, drained of energy. I rolled down the windows and rested my cheek in the cross flow of air.

I seemed to be at some sort of junction: on the one hand staunchly anti-gun, on the other, apparently very easily seduced by close personal contact with the enemy. Perhaps I was living that slogan from the pro-gun literature, *people not guns are the problem*.

—

Of course it is possible to fall in love with the apparatus and its history. My reading had led me to Ambroise Paré and his 1634 treatise, *Of Wounds made by Gunshot, Other Fierie Engeines, and all sorts of Weapons*, where the paragraphs on the origins of gunpowder and the 'new Engeine which we terme a gun' were as deeply fascinating as Paré's own negative attitude to firearms of all kinds.

'I think the deviser of this deadly Engeine,' he wrote, after many harrowing years as a battlefield surgeon, 'hath for his recompense, that his name should be hidden by the darknesse of perpetuall ignorance, as not meriting for this

his most pernicious invention, any mention from posterity.'

Later I found a quote I'd copied into my notebook while reading V.S. Naipaul's *Half a Life*.

> But then, to my great surprise, I was entranced the first time I looked down a gun-sight with a finger on the trigger. It seemed to me the most private, the most intense moment of conversation with oneself, so to speak, with that split-second of right decision coming and going all the time, almost answering the movements of one's mind. It wasn't at all what I was expecting. I feel that the religious excitement that is supposed to come to people who meditate on the flame of a single candle in an otherwise dark room was no greater than the pleasure I felt when I looked down a gun-sight and became very close to my own mind and consciousness. In a second the scale of things could alter and I could be lost in something like a private universe.

IT WASN'T UNTIL THE NINETEENTH CENTURY, when science and medicine turned their ears to the pleas of the psychologically wounded, that a systematic exploration of 'trauma' began. The word itself is Greek and means *wound*. It still means *wound* in a flesh and blood sense, but it also means 'a startling experience which has a lasting effect on mental life; a shock'. In 1889 Pierre Janet observed his patients continually reliving their original threat, never learning that the threat had gone and it was safe to stop being vigilant. These people could not function as integrated citizens in the here and now of their lives because they were haunted by the snarling dogs of the past. Janet wondered if the emotion supporting and heightening the original threat was so overwhelming that it re-routed the laying down of memory to some other place; for example, he wondered, could the memory become locked into the body itself, the cells, or into the eyes (so causing nightmares and flashbacks)?

It is becoming common in today's world to bring victims and perpetrators together after a traumatic event. In the absence of an identified shooter my fears had been displaced onto, or forged with, the gun itself. So it was fitting that we meet and exchange addresses, and even hint at romance ahead.

The theory behind the practice seems sensible enough: the initial meeting (in which an act as horrific as rape or as stupid as vandalisation of property might have occurred) is reengineered, this time in a controlled setting, with an adjudicator, a referee, safeguards, and rules of conduct. Rules are part of the set-up and even if the meeting erupts in recriminations with bitterness on the side of the victim and only steely silence from the perpetrator, even then the very thing every victim fears, that is, a repeat of the original assault, cannot happen in a hermetically sealed interview room. Like an arranged marriage, these two people are brought together by third parties to size each other up, and perhaps, just perhaps, see the other party as a human being.

What has changed is the individual's right (in the developed world anyway) to insist on being heard: to say, 'I suffered when I was abused as a child and I suffer now', or 'I was angry and afraid during the war and I am angry and afraid still'. In neurological terms, confronting a feared object or situation is a way of forging a new pathway or circuit in the cortex of the brain, one that equates, say, guns, with a feeling of safety, or even cautious take-it-or-leave-it diffidence.

These new circuits are add-ons, they do not extinguish the old amygdala-based fear zaps. Telling yourself you're not afraid will work, the cortex *can* damp down the terror spasms rising from the old brain, but when the pressure is on, the plane is bucking in high turbulence or a madman in a supermarket points a gun at your head, and the stress hormones flood in, nothing is guaranteed.

—

Target shooters, what we call *sporting* shooters, are the largest group of private handgun owners in this country. Their organisation is looked upon favourably by the police because they know that the association operates under formal guidelines, and that new members have to undergo a course of instruction. In one of their many publications I read:

> Would-be members can be observed closely. Anyone who appears to be a hazard, or to have an ulterior motive, or who will not accept the discipline of regular competition shooting will not qualify.

Australia has 750,000 registered gun owners and over two million registered guns. To become a gun owner the legal way, an aspirant has to join a gun club and be vetted by the establishment, but this checking system extends only as far as the gun owner's activities within the building. If he's acting strangely at home or work, privacy laws prevent it being reported; and limits on police access to a suspect's medical history, and the useful information worried relatives or neighbours might tender, mean that a number of potential harm-doers carry legal guns.

In a follow-up phone conversation with Jean I told her I'd been shooting at the range.

She said, 'Gun clubs are a bit wary of people who tell them they've been shot. Most of the regular guys I've met in my training are very nice sensible people, but they don't want to meet someone who's been shot because of the current attitude to guns in society. Your being shot is a bat for the other side. They were probably thinking, are we training this woman so she can go and shoot the guy back?'

—

About two months after my visit to the shooting centre I put myself in another confronting gun situation, perhaps to test my nerve, but also to see first hand the other face of gun culture, the users who disdain gun clubs with their suggestion of regulated practices. Escorted by my husband, I went to the Arms Fair at a racecourse south-west of Sydney. In a pavilion normally dedicated to the social and domestic needs of race-goers (it has a cafeteria, rest rooms, seating, generous views sheltered from the weather, and a large domed mingling space for punters), were set out stands and trestle tables and all manner of display equipment, so that visitors, after paying an entry fee, and subjecting themselves to the scrutiny of a guard, could inspect what was for sale.

We did a lap of the room, then proceeded up one aisle and down the next to get our bearings, noticing stands we wanted to return to along the way, getting a feel for the sort of patrons who would attend an arms fair.

There was a lot to notice.

I had a notebook at the ready, to record my impressions, but the first thing I did was put it out of sight. My husband, a photographer, kept his bag firmly closed. Tacitly we understood that, even with permission, our anthropological approach would be about as welcome as a television crew looking for scandal to dish up on the evening news. The patrons were almost exclusively male. Any women I saw had on combat shirts, or seemed to be trying to disappear under baseball caps and unisex clothing. I saw one cowgirl. She worked at a stand advertising a Wild West experience and had the full regalia, including big hair and tassels.

To solve my note-taking problem I worked out a strategy. I idled up to an interesting exhibition, like the juxtaposition of the One Nation stand (with their banner supporting gun ownership) plonked directly opposite the Nazi souvenir stand, then strolled into the ladies' room to scribble a note. I don't know if anyone noticed my frequent visits to the amenities, and frankly I didn't care. My overwhelming desire was to take a lot of word snapshots and leave as soon as possible.

The books, as always, drew me in and I leafed through *A Gentleman's Guide to Pig Sticking* and *Better Ways to Clean Your Gun*, intermittently peering at a collection of hunting trophies. I held the dead gaze of a once handsome fox, resigning myself to the knowledge that where there are foxes there will always be fox hunters; but I couldn't make any sense at all of the Pacific turtle in its glass trophy cabinet.

Down the aisle to my right I caught a glimpse of a woman breastfeeding her baby. She must have been the wife of the stall-holder and had found a tiny space behind the display to attend to her child. With my nose in a second-hand copy of *Live to Ride*, a 'bikers' lifestyle mag', I angled myself to watch the exquisite intimacy of a child at the breast. This glimpse of nurturing ameliorated a lot of what I felt was wrong about this place and what it stood for.

My husband returned from an expedition to the music stand. He'd been listening to 'Tank Song 8' from the Rhine Watch collection and had had enough. Was I ready to leave? I pointed out the mother-and-baby scene as we passed, and was on the point of saying something about the redeeming quality of birth and growth, when I was stopped by an alteration to the picture. From this angle we could see the baby's head repositioned, by a perspective shift, into a target for six rifle barrels displayed for sale. The pale roundness of that lovely head looked like a soft and vulnerable fruit.

—

It would be easy to become discouraged about the impact of guns in our modern world. Constantly exposing oneself to their presence creates an exaggerated sense of menace. So I consulted some sources to test my own perspective.

I learnt that in the USA about one million people die each year from heart disease. Just over 11,000 die from gunshot wounds. In Australia, that rate is much, much lower. Against the 50,000 or more heart disease related deaths, around sixty to seventy people die annually from being shot, which is actually five *less* than died in 1968, the year I was wounded.

Even when we add up all the figures, all the wars, all

the armed hold-ups, firing squads, duelling Russians, farming accidents, suburban snipers, gang wars, and firearm suicides, the numbers don't come anywhere near the toll taken by assaults from within our own imperfect bodies (the sudden occlusion of a heart vessel, the stealthy rupture of boundaries by roving cancer cells), and the impact of motor vehicle accidents.

A gun doesn't even have to be fired to achieve a result ('hand over the money'; 'stop right there'). A gun is often a means to an end, a signal that the human holding the firearm has the upper hand.

The television news and the evening papers tell us, in capital letters, that gun crimes are on the increase, yet the mortality figures don't bear this out. What is increasing is the visibility of guns, and the brandishing of guns (real, and duds that look real) in criminal activity. Who but a fool is going to say no to a gun?

—

I applied to two hospitals for copies of my medical records. Blacktown, where I was taken after the shooting, had no paperwork pertaining to me prior to 1976, when I was admitted with chest pains. Totally disbelieving, I attempted to go over heads, calling in old favours from my days of working in hospitals and acting as if sheer force of will would produce my notes. I paid thirty dollars for a single sheet of paper that recorded that in 1976 I'd been given an ECG, was as healthy as a horse, and had been discharged two hours after arriving; and even though the word NO is circled next to the box marked *First attendance?*, there are no old notes stapled to the back.

I had to resist an impulse to storm the barricades and go look myself. My memory of record keeping in days gone by (at other hospitals) is of dusty corners where no one wanted to scrabble around after a hard-to-find document, or of certain staff who were too lazy to look further than the ends of their noses. This was work I would *willingly* do. I still ache to be given the chance. I hold on to the stubborn (though probably erroneous) belief that my file is in there somewhere.

In the meantime I rang the Sydney Adventist Hospital at Wahroonga, where I had slightly better luck. But only slightly. All that remained from my two surgeries to remove the bullet in 1972 and 1973 were the cover sheets. At least I had a dozen or so words of minimalist description to work from.

During 1972, a year of change and hard work for me during which the dramas of the shooting had been overlaid and almost buried, my body had asserted its own memories. I was married in January, began full-time university in March, and in between discovered the huge burden that I'd unwittingly taken on in agreeing to partner my husband in his first business venture, a service station.

After two years in a blue TAB uniform, I now dressed in a blue Mobil uniform to pump petrol before and after a full day at university. In the evenings, I sat in a cold office that smelled of petrol and grease, and added sales figures on a large balance sheet, with one eye on a physiology text book propped against the girlie calendar.

Towards the end of the year something happened to my health. I still had back pain – the odd sharp twinge over a steady dull ache that I was so used to I thought of it as background noise. But I began to get other aches, colicky stomach pains, vague pains in my legs. I lost weight. My headaches got worse. I became irritable, sleep was even harder to manage. The family doctor prescribed Valium – the seventies cure-all – and told me to slow down.

One evening my parents came by the garage to fill up

their car and, finding me distressed, weepy, and unable to unscrew the petrol cap, took me back to my house where I cracked, crying as I rarely do, like someone totally out of control.

I justified my agitation as an accumulation of pressures: end-of-year exams, getting behind in the business paperwork, the travelling between home and university along Parramatta Road, not enough sleep.

'See a doctor,' my mother said.

When I said I had, she held my hands and looked me in the eye: 'See a *good* doctor, or your father and I will step in.'

So I found a GP, a young woman new to the district. She ordered a blood test and, a day later, phoned, asking me to come and see her. The test showed a surprising result, an unusually elevated lead level, along with the anaemia she'd suspected. At this second meeting I told her about being shot three years before, a revelation that might seem like a glaring omission on my part – an event like that ought to have been laid out with emphasis when I gave my medical history – but I was sick of the shooting subsuming everything else in its path. Tonsils out at ten, shot at seventeen ... the history-taking usually stalled right there, and the retelling took up the rest of the consultation.

It was obvious I'd brightened up the doctor's morning. She went away to find a couple of textbooks. Retained bullets. Lead poisoning. It must have beat the hell out of croup or fungus under the nail.

Why didn't the hospital remove the bullet? she wanted to know when she came back. I told her about *pax Romana*.

'But you have a lump of lead in your stomach.'

'They told me the body would grow a case around it.'

'Maybe, but bathed in body fluids, the lead can leach out.'

The next day I was sitting in the office of a surgeon, a

dapper man with, I was fascinated to watch, a fine tremor in his right hand.

On the twenty-first of December I was admitted to a private hospital and underwent a long surgery that came to nothing. *Exploration of back for foreign object*, says the cover sheet. RESULTS: *Unrelieved*. On Christmas Eve, sore and unwell, I was discharged on the proviso that I rested and took antibiotics.

In early 1973 I went back to the same private hospital to be X-rayed with a piece of new technology – a machine whose name I used to know because it was mentioned so often but have since forgotten, or sublimated – and was taken to a suite where the staff seemed to be having a lot of fun with their new toy. Lying on my back I was able to see my abdomen up on a screen (two-dimensional X-rays were all that public hospitals could offer at the time) and there, moving up and down as I breathed, was the bullet. I had to hold my breath, let go, hold again, and all the while a man drew marks on my skin with a thick felt pen. I felt like a dress pattern.

During this second surgery, which was longer and definitely more painful in the post-operative stage, the foreign object was located and removed from something called the 'omentum'. The surgeon gave me the bullet in a glass bottle to take home.

—

Here you are, Hamer, I thought, here's your bullet. Come, sit on my hospital bed now and tell me you think I'm a liar.

There was no fanfare, no one left to care. The case had long been closed.

And yet my body, it seemed, had been going about its own business – silently waging a war against the decisions of professionals.

The literature only records a few cases of death by lead

poisoning from a retained bullet. Certain body fluids are capable of dissolving lead and sending the toxic solution, via the bloodstream, to sites where it can cause disruption and, ultimately, brain swelling.

Reading of a case where a woman died five months after being shot in the leg, I was struck by the fact that though she was hospitalised for severe anaemia, weight loss and abdominal pain, 'a diagnosis of lead poisoning was never considered'. It was only at post-mortem that the tell-tale histological lesions were discovered and her blood tested for lead.

—

At the end of 2002, at a time when my curiosity about the secret life of the human body had climbed a new peak, I requested permission to observe a surgeon at work. Having read that my bullet had been discovered in the *omentum*, I found myself wanting to see this body part in its natural home. As it turned out, I was given a piece of omentum to hold in my hands.

AS BODY PARTS GO, the omentum is a real ugly duckling: a vile-looking apron, studded with lumps of fat, described by Henry Gray, lecturer in anatomy at St Georges Hospital, in his famous reference work of 1858, *Gray's Anatomy*, as *cribiform*, or sieve-like, in appearance. Gray thought its usefulness might be likened to that of a blanket, draped over the intestines to keep them warm. The surgeon I was to observe removing this particular omentum, Dr Monro, told me he thought the omentum had once had a duty (in pre-antibiotic days) something like a field medic who comes to the aid of a stricken comrade and wraps him in layers of warmth and insulation while he heals (or dies). He used different words of course. During an operation surgeons rarely speak in metaphors.

You would almost think humans in the first world could dispense with their omentums, yet each newly minted infant comes equipped with one (in fact more than one, the greater omentum has two lesser cousins) to have at the ready, like an inbuilt supply of emergency bandages, or organic bubble plastic.

I'd had a preview glimpse of the omentum in *A Colour Atlas of Human Anatomy*, lent to me by a medical friend, and through her intervention I now had the opportunity to observe Dr Monro at work on the abdomen of a man whose stomach had to be mostly removed because of cancer. This generous man, the patient, had agreed to my presence in theatre. I was told about his condition during a briefing in the tea-room where the surgeon drew me a diagram and asked me what I wanted to get from the experience of watching abdominal surgery. I was hoping he wouldn't ask me that question. What could I say? – something about trying to understand how the organs fit into the cavity, and what exactly constitutes the abdomen. Luckily he was a busy man with many things on his mind.

'To learn,' I could have said. That would have sufficed. Students observe masters in order to learn.

Dressed in surgical scrubs and feeling like an actor in a television drama, I entered the theatre in the company of the head nursing sister, an admirable lady called Trish, who inducted me into the protocols. Wide-eyed above my mask, I attempted to be as noticing as I could, taking in the colour scheme, the radio music, the sign reminding staff there was a patient on board ('be courteous'), the instruments laid out, the humming sense that something was about to happen.

'If you feel faint,' said Trish, 'tell me. Step back. There's no shame.'

At ten minutes past the hour the patient was brought in, a very pale man in his sixties. I willed myself not to, but I met his gaze and nearly lost my battle for serenity there and then. His eyes were wells of fear, large and dark, and I felt a pull like a tidal force sucking me into his skin. I was sure he was thinking: Is this the rehearsal for the big sleep, the final breath, the descending curtain when cancer finally wins?

'Thank God for midazolam,' said Trish, noticing my noticing.

Blinking, I brought my attention back to her and the room steadied on its pins again.

'Amnesia can be a good thing sometimes.'

When the man was out ('Going to sleep now,' said the anaesthetist, depressing the plunger on a syringe) there followed a lot of manoeuvres: inserting a catheter, applying compression devices to his calves, and – at the top end – putting in an airway and getting his level of unconsciousness right. This was fascinating work to watch. I relaxed into my observer role and made a note. An old song I've always liked came on the radio, 'Does Anybody Really Know What Time It Is?', and mentally I sang the next line. Who is that, I wondered. I should know. I used to know all the singers of all the songs, once.

Now the surgeon had entered the theatre and was standing to one side in a purple gown.

Trish motioned me to move. As I found a spot where I'd be out of the way I saw the anaesthetic nurse put a sheet of clear plastic over the patient's face before draping him completely in green cotton. The shock of it caught in my throat. He will suffocate surely. I made a mute appeal to Trish.

'We're keeping him warm,' she said. She showed me the warming blanket, the hose pumping heated air and explained how the body's core temperature drops unless aggressive measures are taken. But what about the plastic? 'The tubes are breathing for him.' This didn't cheer me. My mind manufactured an image of a blue face stuck to smothering plastic.

Trish repositioned me to watch the initial incision. Under the green drapes the patient was now only a rectangle of bare stomach, and a left arm supported by an armrest.

On a given signal the team stepped up to the plate. The surgeon, his registrar, his resident, a medical student, a student nurse, myself, Trish, the scrub nurse, the anaesthetist, his nurse, and two students: a dozen people all focused on this man's body, the patient anaesthetised on the table.

Being tall I was able to see quite well. The surgical registrar and the scrub nurse stood on small platforms. There is quite a bit of work involved in getting into the abdomen and, once there, quite a lot of blood to soak up and siphon off. The surgeon pointed out fixtures as he went along: the omentum lying over the top, the gall bladder, the pancreas. The man's liver had been affected by other treatments and I craned over to see what was being shown, thinking – as I strained not to intrude too far – how fluid the landscape of the abdomen is, how slithery and wet its contours. I tried not to think of offal and sacrificial entrails, but of course it was all I thought of, because we know this landscape from films and butcher's shops and the current spate of surgical dramas on television, and nothing is sacred any more from the prying gaze of the curious.

Trish drew a diagram on the whiteboard showing how the section of stomach would be removed and stapled all in one movement, using a purpose-built instrument. All the while the scrub nurse fed a line of clean swabs up to the gaping hole and fetched them back again, plumped and bursting with blood. Five at a time they were counted into plastic bags, tied, and the bags hung in a row on a line, like shameful washing.

When I moved to the anaesthetist's end I learnt the reason for this gruesome display: each bag represents a fraction of the total blood loss and has to be added to the amount in the cylinder at the end of the suction line, which as we spoke was at the one-litre mark.

'How many litres of blood in the human body?' the anaesthetist asked me.

God, I should know that. Eight?

No, five.

Trish had been educating me about the anaesthetist's role. He is the big picture man, the person with his eye on the machines, the blood loss, the fluids going in, the length of time the cavity has been open to the air. I think she was telling me he wasn't just an accessory to the surgeon.

The two main men consulted each other. A bag of blood

went up. Two hours passed. My back ached. And it was while I was distracted, examining the intricate tubing that kept the patient stabilised, that I missed it – the actual resection of the stomach.

But Trish called me to put on a pair of surgical gloves and move to the other end of the room. And this is when I took the man's omentum in my hands, getting the feel of its knobbly surface and seeing its points of attachment. Trish then took a pair of scissors and cut the flesh in my hands, at the perimeter, opening it out like a purse to show the stomach lining.

'And this is the cancer,' she said. Several heads joined mine to peer at the malignancy. 'Secondaries,' she explained. And I thought, Is that all? A cluster of what looked like large warts, and a thickening around the pylorus. I'd imagined something black, like a funnel-web spider in the strike pose. The emptying end of the patient's stomach had been blocked by this misshapen tissue. Now he would be able to eat again, albeit smaller portions.

Once the new connections were in place and the extra blood sluiced from the cavity, the sewing up began, followed by stapling and a covering plaster. The surgeon left and the audience dissipated. Theatre, for us at least, was over.

In the scrub room I seized the moment to whip up the front of my tunic and show the surgeon my old scar. Please tell me what you can, retrospectively, I said. My timing was off.

The medical student who had been standing near me during the operation pushed in through the doors just as my clothing settled and the surgeon, who had only a few minutes to give me before rushing away, had begun a high-speed re-run of surgery circa 1972. The student, thinking the discussion concerned the man in the next room, asked politely to be included. We turned on his eager young face like parents interrupted by a child. 'This is another matter,' said the surgeon. I saw the young man's expression waver. He held onto courtesy but couldn't restrain disappointment. We left him standing by the sinks. Your moment will come, I thought, you are still young.

I hurried after the surgeon. We found an empty office, I got out my notebook and he dictated. The area of the omentum is above the retroperitoneum, which in turn sits above the pancreas and some major blood vessels. It was indeed miraculous, he commented, that major damage wasn't done to my pancreas – the bullet had been centimetres away from the splenic artery and vein, possibly the aorta, and the vena cava. All big bleeders.

These days, it is practice to go in after every bullet. To clean up the wound, remove dirty, contaminated and devitalised tissue. One looks for nicks in the bowel, or any nick that might bleed slowly, leak, and cause peritonitis.

I had a sudden memory, triggered by his speech, of receiving extra attention one day in 1968 when my temperature went up and I developed a new pain. There was much frowning, and many whispered discussions. More streptomycin, a thermometer every hour, then (I can't remember the time frame) the all-clear. I had not turned septic. Our family are good healers, my mother always said. And we are.

Now the surgeon told me about a farm accident. The bullet had entered the man's body through the abdomen and exited through the buttock. The entry wound was handsomely cleaned up, but the exit wound was barely treated. The buttock became gangrenous.

As I drove away that day I wondered, as I've wondered many times, about the decision to leave my bullet to its own devices, with no surgical attention for an indefinite period, given the possibilities for mutiny inside the undulating serpentine world of the abdominal cavity.

—

Some of the earliest records of the surgical treatment of gunshot wounds are the invaluable written accounts of surgeons working on battlefields, 500 years ago. The first guns were awesome contraptions, monsters of noise and smoke, difficult to load, harder to aim, and brutal in their impact on flesh and bone. Field surgeons found themselves confronted with a new kind of wound: the gaping, infected kind with significant tissue destruction that often demanded improvised treatments.

Hieronymus Brunschwig, one of the first to publish on 'The Noble Experyence of ... Surgeri' in *Chirurgia* (1497), described a two-part approach: first he drew rope through the wound to scour and physically abrade all sides of the bullet track, then he applied a hot fatty drawing substance like bacon or earwax to 'drawe out ye venym'. Supplies permitting, the wound was then wrapped in linen dipped in a salve. If the soldier fell in a field his wound was washed in the nearest goat's or cow's milk.

Retained pellets were removed by 'cuttynge', making an incision wider than the bullet track and inserting a probe-like instrument to grasp the bullet. Brunschwig also describes a bizarre self-inflation method for extracting a bullet from a hard-to-get-at place. The patient is tightly girdled then admonished to strain his veins and sinews to push the pellet outwards until it can be seen pressing 'unto the skynne of the belly' and so extracted by an incision at the point where it surfaces.

In Brunschwig's day gunpowder itself was considered to be a poison and its toxic nature the cause of the red, hot swellings that quickly followed penetration by a musket ball. Soldiers routinely drank gunpowder in wine before battle to build up their resistance to gunpowder poisoning.

To neutralise the poison, 'oyle of Elders scalding hot, with a little treacle mixed therewith' was poured on the wound, a practice which subjected many men to hours of agonising pain and left them scarred.

About eighty years after Brunschwig, Ambroise Paré, who had trained in Paris, challenged the hot oil theory, and the idea behind it that gunpowder was a poison. 'The difficulty of curing proceeds,' he wrote, 'not from the venerate quality of the wounds, nor the combustion made from the gunpowder but the fouleness of the patients' bodies and the unseasonableness of the aire.' Paré asked old country women for their healing recipes, and investigated the composition of gunpowder to satisfy himself of its non-toxic ingredients, along the way trouncing the idea that manufacturers soaked bullets in poison. He began using egg-white and oil of roses, and, after studying under a senior surgeon, adapted his formula for a healing balsam with the strange inclusions of boiled whelps and earthworms, mixed with oil of 'lillyes' and Venice turpentine.

Medical and surgical competence advanced under the influence of pioneers like Paré, with a continuous stream of discoveries, each flowing forward, one upon the other.

The strangely beautiful illustrations of instruments that accompany the old texts remind me in a perverse way of the firearms themselves. Engraved, metallic, elongated, they mirror the barrels down which bullets hurtle. During a visit to the Metropolitan Museum of Art, New York, I once spent a lazy hour examining gun workmanship in the Russell B. Aitken Gallery. Between 1844 and 1862 gunmakers showed off their talents at a series of exhibitions in Paris and London, and looking at a cross-section of their work I could disengage the gun-phobia loop in my head and appreciate the skill in combining steel, walnut and silver, or steel, ebony, gold and silver into very handsome objects indeed. I could not imagine these *objets d'art* being fired. They had no relationship to gunpowder or mangled flesh.

In Paré's *Workes*, I found the forerunners of all the sophisticated surgical implements that modern surgeons rely upon. Here is the 'straight Crane's bill, being also toothed, for drawing forth haile-shot, pieces of armour, splinters of bone, and such things as lye deepe within'. And the 'Ducks bill [which] hath a large round and toothed cavitie in the end, for so it more easily taketh hold of the Bullet when it lies among the Flesh'.

I examined some of these bullet extractors (or *catch-bullets*, as Paré called them) through glass in the museum of Surgery in Edinburgh last year. I longed to pick one up, for the tactile pleasure of operating its moving parts. I was one of two visitors at that moment, and the genial receptionist, a senior gentleman with the air of a retired medical man (which I suspect he was), had happily escorted me to the cabinets that held the museum's ballistics and field surgery collection. How indestructible the instruments of death can be, I thought, as I looked at bullets that had been fired centuries ago.

Thwarted in my desire to touch, I waited until the coast was clear and pulled out my camera, hoping to capture at least one memento of a particularly fine bullet-extractor. Cameras were forbidden but like an impulsive shoplifter I over-rode all my good training and bent to line up a shot.

'*Excuse me*,' rang out a sharp female voice, and I blushed crimson.

My shop detective turned out to be the curator of an upcoming exhibition. She had arrived on rubber-soled shoes, her hands full of posters.

Drawing myself up to my full height, I faced her and spoke a sentence containing the words *author*, *guns*, *history* and *surgery*, which, judging by the expression on her face, had been distorted by some invisible translator into *cretin*, *thief* and *interloper*.

'Transparencies,' she said, accenting each syllable, 'may be purchased at the office. By arrangement.'

I stowed my camera, nodded my rebuked head and made for the door. My friendly guide made soft, apologetic eye-contact with me.

'Here,' he said, loading me up with brochures.

—

One day when I was going through my notes I looked again at part of Wendy O'Shea's medical report. Her bullet wound was classified as 'perforating', meaning the bullet had passed completely through her shoulder. Surgery involved debriding the wound track, and repairing ruptures to tissue and nerves. Significant damage had been noted. Turning the page I saw Dr Monro's name – the surgeon who had let me watch him operate. It took a second for the connection to glow with meaning. In casting out my lines for shooting victims and their medical rescuers I'd never expected to catch a matched pair.

The wound repairers, like the gunmakers, plied their specialist trades at either end of the bloody business of shooting. What a waste of hard-won, expertly conjured dexterity, I thought.

Re-reading Paré, I found this sentence: 'These fire-spitting engeines doe no more spare man, than they doe other creatures, and kill without difference from whence soever they come.'

Metal and flesh. No contest.

THE CONVICTION THAT MY BEING SHOT was a random act dished out by an indifferent universe had survived intact since 1968. It had grown its own hard shell and lodged in a buried part of my brain, sealed off from the worrisome intrusion of the frontal cortex that has to *know* and understand. Then, as these things happen, I lost my footing one day and fell down a hole.

At work in 1994 I heard a news broadcast on our small portable radio. The jury was still out on an unusual case: a crime committed in March 1968. A girl had been murdered, her body buried in a shallow grave in a place 'west of Sydney'. My heart performed what is called a lurch. I tried to listen above the drone of a computer print-out, straining over the words. But I missed some of it.

I was sure the newsreader said the girl had been 'shot'. I scribbled down the date. *Six weeks before me*. The place *ten miles further west*. The rest of my day was blown to pieces. In my head a whole new circuitry began hooking up connections, linking the murdered girl, Helen, the accused man (whom I am legally constrained to rename, and will call Francis Friar), the lonely road I was *sure* she walked home on – my lonely road – the correspondence of dates, *the twenty-six year gap in apprehending the shooter*. The linkages snapped into place. They were almost audible. I became highly aroused. I felt I must be glowing or shining, that every eye must be on me, that the whole world must be watching me suddenly, belatedly, wake up to the fact that I was the escaped victim of a serial killer. Everyone knew but me. Everybody had *always known*. That bastard Hamer, he must have known. The present moment lost its imperatives. There was danger in the air. I had to get a grip, not let my colleagues see how shaken I was. I had to keep doing my job *as if nothing had happened*. Keep my mouth shut. Wait. Watch.

In short I slid on a banana skin into galloping paranoia.

—

When the hour came round again I hunched over the radio like a spy waiting for secret signals. I skipped lunch. I felt ill, seasick, betrayed.

What had scarcely seemed possible – that my belief in the anonymity of the act against me could be overturned by *anything*, let alone an item of news – was not only happening, it was moving like a mudslide, obliterating the landscape, the signposts, and the safe houses of the last twenty-six years.

With my pen flying I wrote down exactly what the newsreader said, and he didn't say 'shot'. He said 'murdered'. Well, I reasoned, murdered can mean shot. The next day I rushed out to buy a newspaper.

> JURY FAILS TO DECIDE IN MURDER CASE
>
> A jury failed yesterday to reach a verdict in the trial of a man charged with the murder of a teenage girl in western Sydney 26 years ago. After deliberating for 21 hours, the jury was discharged when it announced it could not reach a unanimous decision. The nine-woman, three-man jury had been sitting on the trial of Francis Friar, 53, who pleaded not guilty to murdering 17-year-old shop assistant Helen Harrison in March 1968. Ms Harrison disappeared while riding her bicycle from the store where she worked in Pitt Town, in Sydney's far west, to her home at Maraylya, several kilometres away. Her semi-naked body was discovered a week later in a shallow grave at Kurrajong. Despite

extensive inquiries, police could not find the killer and the case was closed.

Friar had been charged back in 1991 after three people told police he'd confessed to killing Helen. One of the three said he'd helped Friar push a light-coloured utility, the car used to pick up Helen, into a creek. Friar accused the trio of telling lies.

The jury at Darlinghurst Supreme Court couldn't decide who to believe. Friar got out on bail and was 'expected to be retried on a date to be fixed'.

My anonymous shooter had a name. All former versions of the story of the night I was shot were now eclipsed, expunged, voided. For too long I'd been barking up the wrong tree, rowing up the wrong creek with the wrong paddle. If Friar was out on bail then I'd better start watching my back.

So this is what happens, I remember thinking. The Big Questions do get answered in an ideal world. If you try to live well and do no harm you're guided towards certain doors.

I rang directory assistance and wrote down a list of telephone numbers. I kept my plans to myself. *Loose lips sink ships*. A saying from somewhere, my childhood? an Ealing Studios film?

The first person I called was a detective mentioned in one of the reports. I said I was worried that Friar might have taken a shot at me in 1968. The detective was brusque, the way professionals are with nutters.

'Friar had a different MO,' he said. 'The Harrison girl wasn't shot.'

I called the Supreme Court, asking about the re-trial. I asked who the defence counsel for Friar was. They wouldn't or couldn't tell me.

This was a bitter, corrosive time for me. There was a biblical, Old Testament vengefulness in the shaping of my thoughts. I set up little scenes for myself: I imagined sitting in a court room slightly off to one side, with a perfect view of Friar. He couldn't see me. He would be listening to the lawyers while I, from my vantage point, would be giving him the evil eye. I plotted his murder. Poison, of course. The water jug. Cyanide-laced cigarettes. Ricin in an umbrella tip.

I still have the folder where I kept my notes from that time. They're the notes of a madwoman. There is heavy use of a neon-pink highlighter pen, a lot of arrows pointing to underlined words in newspaper print, lists of names with more arrows, and three attempts to write an account of the night I was shot. None of these stories gets any further than the first few steps of my walk home. I was incapable of writing what happened next.

In 1994 I didn't find out how Helen had died. The initial jolt of hearing about her murder had left me rattled. For days, weeks, I blundered around plotting my moves, collecting my data, until one day it all just stopped. The madness left me. In the only bit of clear sightedness I exhibited at that time, I judged myself mentally unfit to pursue the matter of Mr Friar.

It would be seven years before I could face Helen's story again, an interval like the fabled seven-year itch, before I could bring myself to travel to the Supreme Court to read several thousand pages of transcript and arrive at an understanding of how Helen's story managed that strange intimate tug that spun me in circles.

—

The Supreme Court building in Sydney has large vertical spaces that dominate the glossy horizontal spaces below. This is architecture that reminds the human spirit about laws greater than its own. Everyone inside moves quickly and with purpose, as though loitering attracts on-the-spot fines. If you hang around on the outside steps (which appear so often on the television news) you see famous faces, news crews, clerks and paralegals having a smoke, and catch a blast of the wind that funnels up King Street like a freight train.

My equanimity was firmly in place again when I jumped through all the hoops required to gain me access to the Helen Harrison court transcripts. The records of the Supreme Court are sealed to the public; however, by making an application to the Chief Justice and waiting for a judge's decision, a 'non-party' to the proceedings may be given leave to view the documents, under Practice Note No. 97.

The brief upheaval of 1994 was so far behind me that I had to remind myself, bumping along in the train, that Friar had once figured in my inner cosmology. I had no ingrained habit of thinking about my assailant and once I'd let Friar go, as it were, I had quickly lapsed into my usual *unengaged* mode. My particular kind of neuroticism is rather like some forms of eczema. For the most part it's stable and invisible. When I'm stressed, or exposed to irritants, it flares up and itches.

Looking out over the broad glinting waters of the Hawkesbury to Dangar Island I thought how, to an outsider, my interest in Helen Harrison would probably seem morbid and melodramatic. I was reading a cheap paperback edition of Edgar Allan Poe's selected short stories (which had such a repellent cover illustration I'd sticky-taped a postcard over it). In the brief introduction, the editor (a professor of American studies at a British university) quotes T.S. Eliot's observation that Poe, though gifted, had a 'pre-adolescent mentality' that dazzles us with its 'wild flights' but ultimately lacks any maturity and is, well (though Eliot doesn't use the word), wearisome. The professor takes up the challenge, lining up Baudelaire, Mallarmé, Apollinaire and D.H. Lawrence for the defence team. He stakes a claim for Poe's 'apocalyptic imagination, his concern for the morbid and the pathological' based on an undeniable human need for society (whatever forces conspire) to randomly produce individuals who will go where the rest of us dare not go – and report back.

This interpretation sat very comfortably with my pilgrimage to the records office. I was morbidly drawn to Helen's death. I am still, now, engaged in meditations on what I found.

—

At Central country terminal I caught a City Circle underground train to St James, walked through the pedestrian tunnel, and emerged near Queen's Square in a swirl of wet leaves thrown up by a cold June wind. Waiting to cross the road I was caught in a rain shower that had passed by the time I reached the other side. People, I observed, frown and draw into themselves when caught out by the weather. I was in the heart of the city in the middle of winter. The dominant colour was black. I thought of Poe's phrase, 'unredeemed dreariness', smiled to myself, and pushed through the heavy doors of the Supreme Court building.

A friendly woman made space for me to sit in a cubicle cut off by a divider from the main business of the records office. On the other side of the barrier two women were working at computers. They were discussing the antics of a barrister whose name meant nothing to me but, like any good eavesdropper, I tuned in while I waited for the file to arrive. At one stage I coughed heartily to let them know I was there and a head appeared over the partition. I said something like, 'Hi, I'm a researcher. I'll probably be here most of the day. Pretend I'm not here.' Patently, that's exactly what they couldn't do. There was a volley of typing, then the sound of their voices receding down a corridor.

The files were huge. I wondered if I could cope with the claustrophobia of a windowless office for the time it was going to take to go through them. To leave this room I had to make an announcement, brave the eyes of busy people on phones, and exit through a heavy security door. Returning, I had to wait at a reception counter until my escort inside recognised me among the applicants filling in forms, then wait again while she punched a code into a pad and activated the door. I looked around for a coffee machine. Sorry, I was told. There was a café I could go to, outside the building.

So with several large sighs, and a roll of peppermints for company, I opened *Regina v. Francis Friar*. I'd prepared myself. I knew this was going to hurt, in some existential way. When my chest tightened I knew my body was getting in on the act as well.

The timeline of the crime went like this: Helen went missing in March 1968. A week later, her body was found. Thousands of suspects were questioned, one of whom was Francis Friar, then aged twenty-seven. Friar had an alibi. He was at home with his parents. A $5000 reward was posted for information. A replica of Helen's pushbike (the real one had not then been recovered) went on display. Eighteen months later Friar was interviewed again after he bragged to a friend about getting away with Helen's murder. The coroner's inquest in November 1969 brought down an open finding.

Then, what should have been the clincher testimony came, in 1977, from Friar's girlfriend at the time. She gave them chapter and verse of Friar's retelling of the way it happened. A second woman also came forward, saying Friar had threatened to 'do' her the way he did the Harrison girl if she didn't submit to his advances. In 1991 two more people came forward with testimony. One man (a co-worker) said Friar told him 'she died under me'. The other disclosed that he'd helped Friar dispose of the car, at gunpoint. After another inquest, two trials and a hung jury, Friar had walked.

—

Helen wasn't shot. The post-mortem could not establish a cause of death. At post-mortem very little was established except that she had been dead for seven days. Owing to the advanced state of decomposition, identification was made from dental and fingerprint matching.

According to Friar's girlfriend, he had driven Helen to an isolated place and, when she screamed, he grabbed her by the throat. He raped her. She 'passed out'. He raped her again. During that struggle Helen died, possibly of fright, possibly due to an epileptic fit. She had been taking anti-epileptic medication since childhood. Friar buried her in a shallow grave, face down. She was wearing only her blouse and bra. He took souvenirs, which he later showed to two people: a watch, her panties.

As I read further into the file I fell into a deep identification with Helen. This could have been me. Was shooting me an alternative chosen over abduction and rape? If the bullet had hit a vital organ and I'd fallen on the road, unheard by the fireman, I might have bled to death and been found the next day when the first commuters came through the short-cut to catch their trains. Even worse, the shooter might have tried to hide my inconvenient body by taking it away and burying it in a shallow grave. Face down.

Helen is the fallen soldier, my coeval, the one who didn't come home. The very detailed description of her life up to the night she died is eerily like my own. We were born in the same year, four months apart, in Sydney hospitals. We are both eldest female children with younger siblings. Aged seventeen, we both left school before graduating. Helen took a job in a general store. I worked for a while as a milk bar attendant, then started at the TAB. She earned twenty-two dollars a week, I got twenty-four. We both went dancing at the Rivoli (possibly to the same dances) at Parramatta on Friday nights. (I met my first husband at a Rivoli dance four months after being shot.) Born into fire signs, we were impulsive and impatient. Six weeks after Helen died, I was attacked.

Helen died, I lived.

I came across a bundle of exhibits. Maps. Witness statements. Photographs. Fearing what I might see, I left the building for a lunch break. I walked to David Jones department store and wandered around looking at winter fashions. On the lower level I avoided eye-contact with the beautiful demonstrators offering perfume sprays and leaflets. I wanted to look at a moisturiser without arousing anyone's desire to *help*. But by the time I left I'd been atomised with at least four different scents.

I had thought the brisk walk and the strong breeze would brush me clean but, as I settled back into my stuffy cubicle, the waves of floral perfume turned me into a human room deodoriser. I reeked.

Excusing myself, I asked for an escort to the public ladies' room. One of the staff said kindly, 'Look, it's miles away. Use ours.' And ushered me through pin-coded doors with instructions on how to find my way back.

While I was washing my neck over the sink, a woman in a severe suit burst in and propped at the sight (and no doubt the smell) of me. Demanding to know who I was and finding I was 'a visiting researcher', she stepped back in a weird parody of someone who's been told she's locked inside a room with an axe murderer. 'How did you get in here?' I said I'd been kindly allowed to use the facilities, which wasn't the answer to 'how', so she asked again. I said I punched in the number the girl gave me. She repeated what I said, slowly, to get it absolutely correct in her mind. Then she performed an elaborate exit, keeping her back against the wall, her front-of-body towards me, never breaking eye-contact until the last second, when she let me have a flourish of triumph look before slamming the door.

Christ, I thought. Men in uniforms will be here next.

As I returned to the cubicle my accuser was so busy kicking arse she failed to notice that the enemy had once again stormed the gate. For reasons I'm yet to elucidate for myself, whenever I get close to material evidence that bounces a bit of light into my own dark spaces, I rub someone up the wrong way. It was quite possible this woman was rallying the forces to have me ejected, so I put my head down.

What I saw in the exhibits file broke my heart.

Helen lay face down in a shallow grave. Her right arm was up and around her head, her forehead partly resting on her right forearm, as she might have lain on the beach to read a book. Her left arm was sharply bent at the elbow. Her legs were pulled straight, suggestive of the way she was dragged into place. The only clothing, her white bra and the unbuttoned floral blouse, were stained.

I had no idea that decomposition set in so quickly. As I read the description of skin slippage and insect infestation I moved through every person's natural feelings of revulsion into a personalised, perpetrator-directed rage.

I read the list of her possessions found some distance away in the basket of her pushbike: Her folded day clothes (she was going through a pink phase – skirt, blouse, cardigan). White sandals. An address book. A handkerchief, perfume bottle. A paper bag with three unused sanitary napkins. A packet of Lemon Delicious Sponge Pudding Mix.

I fixated on the Lemon Delicious. It belongs so poignantly to that time. I've made it. I can taste it.

These very intimate personal possessions fly out of their

private context into many public hands once you are dead. The man who found them (without finding the body) had a perplexed look-through. Then the police gathered and logged them. Then the forensic people had a look. Then the poor grieving family had to identify them. Then the court staff, lawyers, judge, jury studied them.

Frozen in time like a mummy, Helen never emerges from her pink phase, never marries, never negotiates the journey to self-understanding and forgiveness.

Awkward facts clustered on the edges of her story. As a child she suffered from 'vague' turns, diagnosed as slight epileptic tendencies. Her doctor prescribed Phenobarbitone and Mysoline. Her alleged attacker told a mate, 'Everyone knew she took fits.' Yet at the trial Helen's father vehemently denied that Helen was still medicated for epilepsy. He said she'd grown out of it.

Is it possible to die from or during an epileptic fit? Yes, say the text books.

The coroner, bringing down his findings in 1969, wrote:

> … due to the advanced state of post mortem decomposition, the cause of death could not be established. I do not propose to conjecture as to the cause of death. Evidence has been given that the death may have been due to natural causes, or through asphyxiation. It could equally be the case that death was due to a felony. Death may have also been caused accidentally. The actual physical cause has not been established, and cannot be established. Similarly, the place of death has not been established.

And further on,

> It may be that no offence relating to the causation of the death has been committed. Certainly, there has been committed the lesser offence of concealment of a body.

The coroner brought in an open finding. In court, the crown prosecutor stated, 'The clear inference is she met her death by foul means.'

—

The gist of the story of Helen's last hours comes from statements made by her parents, her employer, townspeople, the detectives, the coroner, and the trio that Friar accused of lying. The information is theirs; the composition of words is mine –

Helen rides her bicycle to and from work, a four-and-a-half mile journey she makes twice a day, six days a week.

The day she dies is her half-day, Saturday morning. Helen's in no hurry to leave, this particular Saturday. She hangs around, chatting. This is down-time. She drinks a soft drink, changes into her riding clothes (shorts, a floral blouse), perhaps not noticing the weather, not looking up, thinking instead of the weekend, the dancing, and her secret boyfriend, a man old enough to be her father, an eyebrow-raising involvement if people ever knew.

Everyone who was interviewed about Helen's last day mentions the storm clouds. Her boss, the delivery boy, the locals driving to or from shopping or visits. Pitt Town was rural in 1968. The land was cut into farm-size lots, the roads were silent for long periods. Helen's father, under questioning in court about the route Helen took home, said, 'It was a very lonely road, put it that way, back in 1968.'

So the storm clouds are building and everyone – bar Helen, it seems – has an eye on the sky. Her boss advises her to start riding now to miss the storm.

Back at the family home Mrs Harrison is also looking at the sky. Her husband is having his afternoon nap. They have a ten-acre farm. Mrs Harrison, noticing the clouds, asks her husband if he should pick Helen up, to save her getting wet. Her husband replies after a quick scan of the sky: 'I don't think it'll be much, she'll be alright.'

During two inquests and two subsequent trials Mr Harrison is forced to repeat that ominous sentence with its tragic resonances in front of strangers who might privately condemn him for putting his head back on the pillow.

The nagging battle of parenting springs to mind: Do we mollycoddle? Do we encourage independence? Do we interrupt our naps or the cricket test (or World Championship wrestling) to pick up a teenager with two legs and energy to burn?

Now in her shorts, with her things arranged in the basket attached to the handlebars of her bike, Helen waves a carefree goodbye to her workfriends, and pedals off into history.

Miss Edwards passes, going in the opposite direction. They lift their hands in greeting. Helen turns into Dural Road as the first heavy raindrops splash on her eyelids. In her last hour of life she meets nature in one of its extreme expressions, the heady zing of charged air particles, a thunderclap, the downward push of rain. Maybe for the first time on Saturday afternoon, she too looks at the sky and takes it into her calculations. She might out-pedal the worst of it if she goes through the short-cut.

The short-cut is the disused airstrip. There are two sections, a partly surfaced road, then a dirt strip used by the local boys for drag racing. As she mounts the concrete strip a car pulls around in front of her. She recognises the driver. He's been coming to the shop. He always buys a sandwich and cigarettes, then leans an elbow on the counter. He wants to take her out. He's seen her at the dances, reminds her he's been watching her on the dance floor. In the shop she won't meet his eye. There's something too eager about him, too knowing. She's seen him at the Rivoli in Parramatta, and the

Blacktown Civic Centre. Meanwhile the rain is easing off. It is passing, bowling through like a giant's hand, stripping leaves, shaking trunks, then withdrawing.

'Come on,' he says winningly. 'Get in.'

In the full flush of her power, two weeks before her eighteenth birthday, she lets him put her bike into his car, and confidently climbs in beside him.

Four days later at East Kurrajong, many miles from the disused airstrip, a car pulls off the road. The driver notices a cane basket leaning up against a wild apple tree. Neatly placed on the top of what looks like clothing is a paper bag and a packet of pudding mix. Searching deeper the man finds a pink skirt, blouse, cardigan, and the purses, make-up and diaries. Having heard about the missing girl, he contacts police. It takes two days of searching this dense bushland before they find the grave.

—

When her distraught father is brought to the morgue he cannot identify Helen. Helen's dentist (and a set of fingerprints lifted from a bottle of bubble bath) are the final arbiters of identity. The body has a name and an address.

And so the pieces come together.

Now the scientists have their magic to perform. At autopsy Helen is reduced to parts. But nowhere in this division and examination of the parts is there any clue to the way she died. The government analyst finds no bullet holes, no stab wounds, no poison, and no spermatozoa. No broken bones, no ligature marks, no strangulation, no abrasions, contusions, lacerations, fractures. With no brain to dissect it is impossible to look for gross haemorrhage or small-vessel bleeding.

The analyst can say categorically that Helen is dead. Further than that he cannot venture.

Nowadays a forensic anthropologist would have been called in. The science of decomposed remains has progressed well beyond this exchange, in 1968:

> *Crown Prosecutor*: 'Granted that the deceased had been interred in the ground for about a week, would you necessarily expect semen to be detectable in the vagina if it had been there?'
> *Autopsy Doctor*: 'No.'
> *CP*: 'Why?'
> *AD*: 'Well, the amount of decomposition was marked to that degree which would also cause decomposition in any sperms.'

This was the Pitt Town murder that took Blacktown's best detectives and left Hamer to manage my case. When my incident happened, these officers were compiling thousands of pages of enquiries about Helen, going through interview after interview, staging reconstructions and making public appeals for new leads. At the time of Helen's first inquest, some eighteen months later in November 1969, they were still working for her. The coroner wrote in his summation:

> … the police assure me that investigations are not as yet complete, and they will not regard this case as closed until the cause of death and circumstance relating to same have been established.

During the talk I had with one of these men (the one I wished had been on my case and whose name was Bob), I spoke to him about Helen. I explained that it had been while reading Helen's file that I'd come across his name, but I wanted him to understand that it was more than his name and the possible link to my case that prompted me to go looking for him. I was drawn to him through his case notes. The great respect he showed to the family, the non-judgmental way he dealt with the sensitive issue of Helen's secret boyfriend, the subtext of his 'just the facts' outline of events, the choice of adjectives, his emphasis, all told me he was more than a good policeman. His statement is a small masterpiece of exposition devoid of much of the dead jargon one sees in written policing.

He excused himself, went to another part of the house, and returned with a box of documents. 'I've thrown a lot of stuff away over the years,' he said, 'but I always kept Helen's file.' He showed me a black-and-white photograph, the same one I'd seen in a newspaper. Then others. I wondered if he could possibly know how deeply affecting this was for me, how deep inside the identification I'd gone. Again.

So I asked him, in his professional opinion, could my shooting have been related in any way. Friar had convictions for firearm offences, for robbery, carnal knowledge, larceny, malicious wounding, drugs. He'd done time.

If he'd hung around Helen at the same dances I used to go to, could he have followed me as well, waited, fired?

Bob thought about it and, after saying that anything was possible, arrived at the answer. 'No.'

Friar, he said, liked to stalk his women with charm. On at least six occasions he'd approached Helen, either at the store or the dances, and, when he had her in his physical space, worked his version of animal magnetism on her youthfulness. He got pleasure from anticipation. He was excited by resistance, up to a point, then lost his temper, lashed out. (I remembered a story in the court file, a report from witnesses outside a dance hall who had to call Friar off a girl he nearly strangled when she pulled away from his kisses.)

In the detective's view, there would be no mileage for Friar in wounding me then letting me run away.

He seemed a little sad to be the bearer of bad news.

—

Mr Molomby QC had said at the final trial, 'The ability to get to grips with the detail is lost with the years.'

As I drove away from my meeting with Bob I felt lighter for having rubbed Friar out of the picture. If there was a link, and I prayed there wasn't, the slow corrosion of memory by time had operated positively in my favour.

Back in 1968 I'd given Detective Hamer the name of a boy, my first real boyfriend, who'd got himself into trouble the previous year by taking cars that didn't belong to him. I'll call him Joe. His eighteen months or so of imprisonment (most of it in a low-security centre) had had a sobering effect on him and he emerged from this (unlike so many others) awakened to Christianity and with a determination to stay well away from trouble. He later married, had a large family, and settled in a quiet suburb with a lot of trees. In the years after his release I saw him very occasionally. He once called at our service station to buy petrol and we shared an awkward five minutes making small talk and scanning the sky over each other's shoulders.

Rumours that Joe was implicated in the shooting started soon after the news hit the headlines. I didn't believe it then, and I don't now. The basis for the rumour was an interview I'd given police about Joe's whereabouts on a certain night back in 1967, a circumstance that sent my parents through the roof with angry concern. First I'd left school for no good reason, now I was going out with boys and putting myself in compromising situations. After the police interview I was grounded and told never to go near Joe again. (Soon afterwards, I met the English boy who pleased my parents but would dump me when my shooting made front-page news.)

It was my testimony, according to the conspiracy theorists, that had put Joe in jail. He'd served six months at Long Bay, making number plates, then been transferred to Emu Plains detention centre.

The theorists were of the opinion that six months in Long Bay had been sufficient to taint Joe, to bring him into contact with bad elements, the types who have definite ideas about retribution and could engineer a revenge hit from inside.

A contract shooting? I told anyone who tried this line on me to stop watching so much television.

My memories of Joe are of the purely physical, first-love kind. The colour of his eyes, the softness of the mohair jumper he sometimes wore, his voice, the music we played.

It was with a good deal of throat clearing and hesitancy that I picked up the phone after thirty years and called him one night – not out of the blue, that would have been unfair, but after having a third party who kept in touch ring him first.

My first reaction was: it's not him. The voice on the phone sounded nothing like the Joe I used to know.

Even harder for me was negotiating the minefield of his possible involvement. How do you ask a question like that?

I started in our respective childhoods. We'd been neighbours since I was seven. I told him how I'd gone back to Toongabbie and been confused by so much change. Joe, the outdoors type, had known the creek and the tracks through the bush on the Watson property better than all of us. Had he seen the new shapes of our old houses – I dropped into an intimate, soft-voiced tone – and the widened, fast-transit road with no Dip in sight? Momentarily, I wanted those times back again, before the Fall, as it were.

But Joe was a long way away. The closer I crept the more he retreated.

I got the impression he was keeping his voice down. When I asked, he told me his kids (now grown) knew nothing of his time in prison and, clearly, he wanted things to stay that way.

I dropped the intimate tone and switched to reporter mode. Did Joe know he had been a suspect in my shooting?

Yes. Was he interviewed at Long Bay? *Yes*. Was he given a hard time? *Yes*. How did he hear about the shooting? He couldn't remember, the news, the radio maybe. 'It was a big story,' he said.

Stripped of their context, these questions had the impact of cross-examination. I took a breath.

I need to know if you were involved, I said. *No*. You understand why I have to ask? *Yes*. I'm writing a book, it's stirring up a lot of old stuff. *It would*.

I hear you're a sporting shooter. *Yes*. I went to St Mary's range to fire guns as research. *I go there*.

When I hung up I sat for a while thinking back over our year or so of dating. Sweet thoughts, like the little rush of heat that changed us from buddies to tentative lovers (of the petting kind). Songs. 'Itchycoo Park'. 'Wouldn't It Be Nice'.

Had we ever been as romantic as my memories? I tried coaxing more of these tender scenes from their pink-ribboned box, and knew with a sudden flash of insight that the great first-love thing had in fact been a fairly regulation, lopsided affair. The leaning had come from my side. The pulling away from his.

No, Joe, you didn't send someone to shoot me. That would hint at a crime of passion and, despite the risks you used to take, and the edgy hunter you sometimes let me glimpse, you didn't care enough for me to lie awake at nights in your cell figuring out ways to have me removed from the face of the earth. That's why we broke up.

But I had to ask.

—

The poster at the writers' festival advertised a detective named Ray who would be talking about crime scenes. I claimed a seat near the front and took out my notepad.

Pens, including mine, scribbled madly. *The tell-all corpse. The marks, visible and invisible, left by the killer. The attention of ants, maggots, rigor mortis, dogs, necrophiliacs, bacteria, lime, morticians.*

He showed a series of slides, images that came with a warning. I heard a few gasps behind me, but, on the whole, people who come to these seminars are steeling themselves to write about murder and are already learning the skill of compartmentalising their reactions.

At question time the audience asked Ray things he could get his teeth into. The dos and don'ts of 'reading' a scene for clues. The gross and subtle approaches to evidence. It was all deeply involving, bringing out the best in the audience, and in this man who had so much first-hand experience.

My hand flew up.

'How would police tackle a crime scene where there was no body, no criminal, no vehicle, no witnesses and almost total darkness?' I heard myself ask.

He fixed me with a look, then said something quick and dismissive about every scene having its challenges and nodded to the next raised hand.

The mood in the room skipped a beat, then the crime buffs and would-be crime writers, who had been up to their knees in the blood and gore angle, immediately got back to their good questions, the sort you hear on BBC dramas, and the American television show *CSI*, and my contribution – cutting across the bows like a bit of twaddle from a first-year philosophy student wrestling with puzzles of the 'if a tree falls in a forest and no one hears it' kind – was left hanging in dead airspace. What possessed me to ask an intensely personal question in a public forum when the meaty stuff, bullet calibre and exit wounds, was up for grabs? What had I expected the man to say?

Only afterwards did I understand where I was going with

my question. The tree in the forest made me want to make a case for crimes that leave no corpse and no footprints. The daughter whose bed becomes a temporary crime scene when her father comes home drunk and transgressive. The child who is stalked after hours by playground bullies, where nothing but fear itself is inflicted.

What was it in my own personality, I wondered, that rolled over and played dumb in the presence of law enforcers? Even during the seminar I'd felt something in me shrink from major to minor. Whatever wisdom has come my way over the passage of years, whatever competencies I've earnt, wrinkle like a crepe dress in the rain when I get close to expressing myself, adult to adult, to a policeman. I wanted to shake this girl inside me who wouldn't grow up, the seventeen year old still in thrall to Detective Hamer, the great disappointer.

I solved my dilemma by writing Ray a letter, outlining the circumstances, and asking if he could reconstruct the night I was shot from a police point of view. He was kind enough to reply and we spoke by phone.

There *are* procedures, he told me, for the sort of ephemeral crime scene I described. Tyre tracks, for instance. The shooter revved his car, he might have laid rubber. A spent rifle shell. A witness who happened to be looking out of a car or house window at that precise second, or who heard a bang and noted something: say, the rapid exit of a vehicle. Someone standing on the overhead footbridge at the railway station.

There is always something. Traces. Impressions.

Whether the attending officers attempted to look for physical evidence of the car is unknowable. An entry on the occurrence pad, 'patrolled area, no car found, no witnesses', is not an index, he stressed, of the amount of effort expended. 'They have to cover their backs,' he said. Ballistics would have been informed, but with no gun, and the bullet still in my body, there was nothing to work with.

The things they did have to work with, in the absence of physical evidence, were locked into their brains from years of policing the environment. Each officer would know the local weirdos, hoodlums, gun nuts, flashers and pervs as solidly as any shepherd knows his flock. If firing off shots at young girls late at night was the MO of one of their gun nuts, they would have been banging on his door ten minutes after the call-in. Gun nuts, the detective told me, are sad individuals whose whole lives are taken over by a relationship with a gun, in the way a sick love affair, or a fetish, squeezes everything else out of the picture. With a gun in their hands they transform into heroes, gunslingers, outlaws, cartoon and television characters, sometimes dressing up or taking on a pose – an extension of boys at play that has detached from the make-believe world and grown legs. The really sick ones get a sexual kick out of it.

'My bet is a gun nut.'

ANDY WARHOL WROTE, in *The Philosophy of Andy Warhol: From A to B and Back Again*, 'Before I was shot, I always thought that I was more half-there than all-there – I always suspected that I was watching TV instead of living life ... Right when I was being shot and ever since, I knew that I was watching television.'

During the immersion phase of research on guns and trauma I frequently found myself reaching a flailing hand towards the solid shores of High Art. Where was the literature, the paintings, the music? Poe was there, of course, deliciously morbid, incurably traumatised by death; and the Russians, Dostoevsky, Pushkin, Lemontov; and over there, Graham Greene playing Russian roulette. I found paintings of languid English youths resting on fowling pieces, Sidney Nolan's Ned Kelly series, and much to read about muskets in *Borodino* and *Waterloo*; but my grip never quite held. The current of this snaking river swept briskly by the southbank complexes of the world, and their museums, and only slowed in the press of urban housing and the wide open spaces where silences seem to invite the explosive force of gunpowder.

The 'fierie Engeines', invented for wars and credited with assisting man's quest for honour and glory, tumble from their putative lofty heights once the man in the streets gets his hands on them. Guns today, no matter how you dress them up, are an excrescence of popular culture, and it is in popular culture that all the symbols and icons aggregate.

—

Andy Warhol, pop artist, was shot by Valerie Solanas on the third of June 1968. The .32 bullet went through his lung, ricocheted through his oesophagus, liver, gall bladder, spleen and intestines, and exited through his left side. Pronounced clinically dead, his chest was cut open and his heart massaged manually.

Anyone who cares to can see the patchwork quilting of surgical scars on Warhol's torso in the famous Richard Avedon photograph, first exhibited in New York's Marlborough Gallery in 1975, and now reprinted in magazines and on the internet. In an essay accompanying the original exhibition, art critic Harold Rosenberg wrote, 'Avedon's camera refuses to confer poetry or distinction on his painters, writers, and other famous personages.'

Warhol's face, and his body below the waist, have been cropped out of the picture. His right hand seems to be fingering his scars (which were nearly twelve months old at the time) while his left hand folds down what seems to be a stretch-fabric belt, the better to highlight the extra navel created in his left abdomen by the exiting bullet.

The pop artist known for his confronting filmic images of the sins of the flesh is offering the camera yet another confrontation. The viewer is drawn into a rare intimacy with the aftermath of heroic measures to save Warhol's life from the ravages of a bullet – and we are left with the sure knowledge that heroic measures overlaid the original wounds with ravages of their own.

Warhol is quoted as saying, 'I thought that the pain I'd felt lying on the floor was the worst you could ever feel.' When the ambulance men (who took thirty minutes to get there) put him in a wheelchair instead of on a stretcher, Warhol later said, 'In a sitting position, I knew it wasn't [the worst kind of pain].' Fifteen minutes later, he 'died'.

—

For one of the most powerful popular expressions of 'the kill shot' and all its ignoble repercussions, I listen to Bruce Springsteen's 'American Skin (41 Shots)' – from the Bruce Springsteen and the E Street Band's *Live in New York City* recording.

It begins with a haunting hymn-like repetition of the words *forty-one shots* against the background noise of an engaged audience, eager and just a little too restive for Mr Springsteen, who says, after the eighth repetition, 'We need some quiet.' It's not a rebuke, it's a signal to those listening that a serious subject is on the table. You don't have to know the story to be chilled by the message in the song. There is enough in the lyrics and the deep honesty of the delivery to know that someone innocent has died in a hail of bullets.

My husband told me the story. Twenty-two-year-old Amadou Diallo, a West African immigrant living in the Bronx, was killed in the vestibule of his building when he reached into his jacket to take out his wallet. Four police officers fired a total of forty-one bullets at him, believing him to be a rapist they were hunting. Nineteen of the bullets hit Diallo, tearing up his body from four different angles. The police officers were arrested, tried and found innocent – but never lived down the public outrage.

In July 2000, police union officials called for a boycott of Springsteen's concerts. Some people say the song helped change the course of the elections that summer.

—

My flailing hand also reaches for the television control

buttons, the one sure place it's always likely to find a firm, comfortable grip on the idioms of gun culture.

We know their names, the popular gun heroes like Wyatt Earp, Buffalo Bill, Wild Bill Cody and the invented heroes like The Lone Ranger, Dirty Harry, and Rambo. In our house when I was young, the whole family watched *Rawhide* and *The Rifleman*, as uncritical of any underlying message, that guns are needed to solve the really important problems, as the next family watching the same shows.

The legacy of the Wild West, or the Old West, is distilled (for me) in this uncritical acceptance that a man is a man when he's got a gun in his hand. The type of man (preferably handsome, tall, moody) is as important as the type of gun he's carrying, and any modern policeman will tell you that street guns are as much a fashion statement as an instrument of intent. Only desperados and domestics grab the nearest piece of firepower.

Wyatt Earp (or, more correctly, the TV version of Mr Earp, actor Hugh O'Brian) popularised the Buntline Special Colt revolver. The Colt was handsome, fast, and 'cool' before the word acquired its colloquial, fashionable connotation. In the longarm category, the Winchester lever-action rifle (the saddle gun) and its descendants claimed the high ground even when better, more efficient models (like the Lee Enfield and Mauser) hit the market. The Colt and Winchester brand names stuck until they were ousted by the next revolution in gun fashion.

The firearms that were definitely 'uncool' right from the beginning and remain in that daggy basket are the .22 calibre long and short, all double-action revolvers, the issue handguns and rifles of soldiers, and the pocket handguns of 'urbanites', the small-time street criminals on the desperate end of the spectrum. Urban warriors with limited funds, and gun nuts with attitude, were responsible for the sub-set of patched-together weapons called gats, heaters, roscoes, and Saturday night specials. In the big gun stakes, the double-barrel shotgun or scatter gun had no street cred in the Old West (it was carried by tenderfoots), but transplanted to a modern urban setting, it soon scared the hell out of anyone in its way.

—

At the time of my visit to the gun fair, one of my objectives was to see for myself what draws people away from the sunshine into a crowded indoor marketplace to brood over all sizes and shapes of guns and the surprising paraphernalia that gathers in their wake. I looked at most of the guns and rifles, probably with less affection than the enthusiast but nonetheless with a measure of baffled intrigue, and then wandered to the book stalls looking for a good general guide to take away and study in cerebral comfort. On my travels around the room I searched for something or someone to tell me more about .22 rifles, the instrument that carried the bullet with my name on it. And in that vast space, where you could buy CDs of Panzer marches from the Third Reich, a beautiful matched set of flintlock pistols in its original case, or visit the Big Game boys with their enormous elephant rifles, I soon realised I was wasting my time looking for evidence of the 'uncool' .22. I asked a man at the book stall where I bought my 1983 *Encyclopaedia of Modern Small Arms*, and was met with a puzzled but trying-to-be-helpful frown. He thought I should try the stall about halfway down the main aisle. He gave me the name of a woman who, I learnt, had her permanent bookshop in a rural town way west of Sydney and tried never to miss these fairs.

For what I thought was a rip-off price of twenty-five dollars, this woman sold me a 1978 softcover edition of *The Gun Digest Book of .22 Rimfire* by John Lachuk. Value, I guess, is in the eye of the beholder, but even if there were black-and-white pictures of Steve McQueen, Clint Eastwood and James Arness aiming .22s in the first ten pages, I felt like a tenderfoot taken for a ride.

Before leaving I visited a stand advertising cowboy action shooting. What attracted me was the woman with big hair and generous bosom dressed in slashed buckskin, spruiking to passers-by about the thrills and spills of playing cowboys in a safe, theme-park atmosphere. I picked up a brochure to add to my reading matter and went back into the sunshine.

Since then I've become very fond of my *Gun Digest*, and have mentally apologised to the bookseller. The opening paragraph tells me in four sentences what the gun world thinks of the .22:

> An informal poll of fellow shooting enthusiasts ... revealed that all but one had begun their shooting careers with a .22 rimfire rifle or pistol. All had 'graduated' into bigbore shooters in adulthood ... The apparent conclusion to be drawn from this pint-sized poll is that the youthful affection for the .22 rimfire that lighted up our formative years, persists throughout our adult lives. [Then] with advancing years, the attributes that made rimfire guns so attractive to our youth again reassert themselves with the enfeebling effects of old age.

Lachuk, a highly respected gun marksman and author, cites an impressive list of famous people who used .22s in their formative years: Annie Oakley (Little Miss Sure Shot) and her. 22 Marlin 1897 Model, Tom Mix and his .22 Winchester, James Arness (or Matt Dillon in his TV persona) and his Remington Model 241 Speedmaster, Roy Rogers and his lever action Marlin .22, and Steve McQueen and his great-uncle's single-shot Stevens 'Crackshot' rifle. I twice read the paragraphs on Rodd Redwing, a full-blooded Chickasaw Native American who was the technical firearms director on many Hollywood Western classics (*High Noon*, *Duel in the Sun*, *Shane*) and coached stars like Marlon Brando, Glenn Ford and Dean Martin. Redwing was a gifted performer, using a Colt single-action army revolver 'sleeved down to .22 rimfire', or a Marlin Model 39 lever-action rifle with no sights, to shoot at small white discs through a two-inch hole in a swinging pendulum. It came almost as no surprise to find he could hit the same white discs through the hole in a Lifesaver mint.

Nearly 150 years after the Wild West was born, it was still alive and kicking here in the suburbs of Sydney. Who, I wondered aloud to my husband, would have thought it? I wanted to know more.

A quick search on a directory showed a list of half a dozen cowboy action shooting clubs in NSW, and others in Queensland, Victoria and South Australia. The types of events offered were: black-powder shooting, Australian Winchester winter round-ups, territorial and range war shooting, Gunfight at the OK Corral days, Silverado shootout days and regular cowboy Western action monthly shoots. Most of the clubs are affiliated with the California-based SASS, the Single Action Shooting Society Inc., whose website makes fascinating reading for the uninitiated. I quote:

> The truly unique aspect of Cowboy Action Shooting™ is the requirement placed on authentic period or western screen dress. Each participant is required to adopt a shooting alias appropriate to a character or profession of the late 19th century, or a Hollywood western star, and develop a costume accordingly. Your SASS shooting alias is exclusively yours. In the tradition of the Old West cattle brand registries, SASS prohibits one shooter duplicating another's alias. There is only one Tex, one Kid Curry, and one Loophole Pettifogger.

I thought of the big-haired woman at the gun fair when I

read, 'The SASS puts a great deal of emphasis on costuming.' This went on to give hints on low-cost ways of achieving the look:

> Visit your neighbourhood thrift stores. Look for lightweight wool slacks with plaid or vertical stripe patterns or old formals, for example. Ladies, take the old satin, silk, or whatever formal, add a little lace, change a hem line, add a feather boa, and a hair comb … voila, you're a saloon girl.

The dress-up, play-acting elements are balanced by a strong emphasis on safety, and the more I read, the more I thought it all looked like good, harmless fun. It seemed to me (though I may be wrong) that the people who would bother to join a club, construct a costume and an alias, and abide by the pages and pages of rules, are hardly the people who might break out of the restraints of a tightly framed organisation to go on a shooting rampage. Although I was troubled for a moment by memories of Wayne O'Shea's killer, who had carefully dressed up in layers of costume (on a very hot day) before killing two people and seriously wounding two others with his .22 Magnum rifle. When asked about his costume, he said he was 'acting a part'.

—

As if on cue to reinforce my growing convictions about popular culture, Channel 7 ran *Thelma and Louise*. In came Susan Sarandon and Geena Davis, reminding me, suddenly, that gun play isn't always a man's game. Right from the outset of my long detour into the world of guns I'd been consulting men, deferring to men, behaving (as my gun history dictated) like a virgin in a pool hall, and only once meeting a sensible, mature female practitioner (in the shape of Jean, the RSPCA officer), who'd shown me another version of the equation linking humans, guns and the extinction of (albeit, animal) life. How had I forgotten *Thelma and Louise*, and the thin but detectable matriarchal line of strong, gun-savvy women stretching back to Annie Oakley and beyond?

I'd remembered the Monument Valley scenery, Susan Sarandon's sunglasses and headscarf, and the arc of their T-Bird car suddenly interrupted in a freeze-frame over the Grand Canyon at the end, but I'd forgotten (or tucked away) the prominence of guns in each of the key scenes.

I know that the cop who pulls them up in Monument Valley is a caricature of every macho bully ever invented, but I've met men like that, I've been pulled over for speeding by a policeman who could have been his brother, and as I lay on the lounge watching Louise play on her feminine charms to win him over (the line I took with my officer), I was reminded of the seemingly inextinguishable notion that a man with a gun is more of a man.

When Thelma stuck her small revolver through the car window and said to the cop, 'Officer, I am so sorry about this. Could you let go of that?' I sat up straight. *Yes!* I wanted to call out. Yes! Change the rules of the game, the game has been in the hands of bullies in uniforms for too long.

This reaction, of course, was an important part of what had made the movie a success.

On the internet I found the text of Callie Khouri's screenplay, and any number of sites selling posters of the girls with their guns aimed at the truck that explodes into a fireball in one of those *kapow* moments in the film. It was strange, I mused, how the dynamic altered when a woman's finger was on the trigger, how I, a gun-avoider and deplorer of the prominence of guns in popular culture, felt the faint shiver of Western gun mystique play over my skin.

'I know it's crazy,' says Thelma the day after they've

locked the cop in the boot and driven off with his gun and ammunition, 'but I just feel I've got a knack for this shit.'

Instead of reading the essays on the significance of Thelma and Louise at their final stand, on the edge of the Grand Canyon, hemmed in by men with superior firepower and plenty of it (displaying, as one author writes, their 'cocked triggers'), I stayed with the girls, thought my way into the moment, imagined how it must feel to go out, guns metaphorically blazing, into the sunset.

Popular writing, comics, movie land and TV land (possibly in that order) are the evolutionary forces that took the rough-edged reality of real gun fighters and shaped them into national heroes with trademark characteristics.

The mystique touches most of us at some time. We watch (or read) and we emulate, and time passes and we move on. Those who don't want the movie to end, but who still want to retain a realistic grip on good citizenship, join gun clubs, or become collectors, or find some hurt-nobody way to indulge their passions. We have nothing to fear, in the main, from devoted hobbyists.

Where the identification turns a dangerous corner is when individuals with bad intentions, or ungovernable tempers, or disturbed mentation reach for a gun to solve a problem because the message *guns solve problems* has seeped into their inner schema through the medium of popular visual entertainment.

Even the pathetic arid zone of the gun nut was once a fertile range where a gun hero leant on his saddle and squinted at the horizon.

FINALLY ONE DAY, the firearms detective I'd been chasing rang me. He was back from assignment in another state and had a free morning. Did I still want to talk?

His voice was business-like, both neutral and guarded. I know that intonation, I use it in my own professional life. As I vacuumed the cat hair off my sitting-room chairs, I hoped the man who was due in fifteen minutes would let me see more than his professional skin. My track record with lawmen had not endeared me to the species. I blamed Hamer for that, but then I blamed Hamer for a lot of things.

Exactly on time, Brendon, a Detective Senior Constable in the State Crime Command, parked his station wagon in my steep, awkward driveway, and I took a peep through the blinds as he came down the steps from road level towards the front door. I wanted to like him, and my first look gave me some hope that we might get off on the right foot.

Close up I felt my heightened tension ratchet back a few notches. This man, I calculated, was my nephew's age. He even looked a little like him. Whether it was an omen or not I took it that way and smiled as I made a pot of tea.

We got straight down to business.

He'd come with a briefcase that he rested on the table near him and never once opened. I wondered what it held – a gun? A tape recorder? Confidential files? He waved away the biscuits and barely touched the tea, but every bit of him was present and ready to interlock with the interview process, with no time constraint, and hardly any caveats on what we might discuss. Of course, I had to stay away from the top secret stuff, but there was no danger of me blundering into covert operations. I'd made avoidance of guns a lifetime vocation.

Brendon had been away working in Queensland on the trail of recommissioned firearms, one of the more common ways for illegal firearms to enter NSW. I was ignorant of the fact that the trade in illegal guns often begins with the legal specimens, which are rendered inactive by a bit of mechanical trickery, submitted for an inactivation certificate, then reactivated by reversing the trickery. The 'new' gun then travels south for hard cash. In a recent sting, a dealer who had recommissioned 6000 guns in this way was caught and prosecuted.

Brendon carries a Glock .40 semi-automatic self-loader. Compared to the Smith & Wesson revolvers of former days, the Glock, according to Brendon, is more user-friendly, more comfortable in the hand and more accurate.

Glocks are popular on the streets now. I'd clipped a piece out of *The Sydney Morning Herald*. An eighteen-year-old Punchbowl youth was facing a possible twenty-year jail sentence for trafficking in guns. A special Strike Force had tapped his phone, intercepting about 700 calls, in one of which the youth was heard to say, 'I am able to get you whatever you want. Forty-fives, you know, nines, the ones the pigs got as well.' He'd been caught selling a Glock and offering to sell an American-made .38 revolver.

Brendon couldn't comment on this case, and I didn't press him. The less I know about street guns, the better I rest. But I was curious about how he relates to his own gun. I'd been asking men I knew (informally) if they played with guns as boys, and how and when (and if) that phase passed.

Brendon's answer surprised me. He claims not to have played with them at all, not even shoot-em-up make-believe with his brother. Not even slingshots. He played sport. His preferred mode is action, and certain aspects of his job, like breaking down doors (which happens less frequently than TV would have us believe; it's more 'knock and announce') satisfy the frustrated footballer inside him. Why then, I asked, join the Firearms Unit?

As his story unfolded I began noticing my own body language. Something remarkable seemed to be happening. Behind my usual props of notebook and tape recorder I was comfortably aligned in my chair, nodding encouragement and generally behaving like someone with a firm grip on her own identity.

—

Of the many topics that we covered, two stand out. The first was a small amusing story about a failed robbery. The robber had entered a service station and approached the console operator with what appeared to be a gun.

'Only it wasn't a gun,' said Brendon, 'it was the top end of one of those trigger garden hoses, painted black and fitted with a bit of pipe to look like a silencer.'

The service station employee, seemingly at great personal risk, made a dive for an internal door and locked himself in the toilet, and the robber, left alone with the goods and money, tried to disable the glass sliding doors to keep away any late-night petrol clients.

'That's where he came unstuck or, I should say, got himself stuck.'

The sliding doors suddenly lunged into the shut position, jamming the robber's head and cutting off the blood flow.

'He passed out, his head stuck outside, his body inside, and the garden hose gun still in his hand.'

I asked him how the service station operator fared, thinking, naturally, of Lisa.

'Oh, he was pretty freaked out,' said Brendon. 'He couldn't see any funny side to it.'

The second story homed straight in on himself, and the reason he transferred out of his former policing job. In more than ten years in the force Brendon has only once pulled out his gun with the intention of using it. And the backlash from that single event had the emotional impact of a head-high tackle.

He was working the back streets of Redfern, trailing a car whose occupant was suspected of a break-and-enter. When he called to the driver (who had run his car into an obstacle) to step out, he found himself looking down the barrel of a shortened shotgun. Instinctively Brendon took aim and fired.

'I missed,' he said. The man fired back then ran away, with Brendon's partner in pursuit.

'All the cars I've pulled over in ten years, nothing like that's ever happened. I've pulled over armed robbers, stolen cars, the lot.'

Clearly this was a watershed moment for Brendon. 'Ninety-nine out of a hundred guys run,' he said. 'It never crossed my mind he'd shoot. We yell, *Police, get out of the car*, and they either freeze or run.'

Afterwards, when the shock set in, Brendon spent sleepless nights reassessing his priorities. He has a wife, young children. All the rehearsals, the dry runs, seemed to have collided with a different sort of reality. At work, he had to go through the safety net of follow-up procedures: a urine test, a breath test, a psych interview, a stress shoot, and a lot of paperwork. He did the stress shoot (in a simulator) with a psych welfare officer watching his every move.

These procedures, which seemed to call his own proficiencies into question, helped in a perverse way to reorient his career towards specialised (rather than general) duties. He transferred to the State Crime Command, into a working life of tracking the shadowy movements of illegal firearms dealers.

Brendon was surprisingly comfortable revealing what might be construed as a failure in performance, and refreshingly candid about his experience of trauma-related stress.

The cluster of characteristics I had come to associate with detectives – bullying mannerisms, ideological rigidity, always having the answers – suddenly relaxed and let in some fresh air.

To sign up for a special task force that operates in the danger zone of gun trafficking, when at the heart of your own core values is an ambivalence towards society's need for guns in the first place, seemed admirable and reassuringly surreal to me.

The next girl who is shot in a dark lonely street could do worse than have such an officer on her case.

I DON'T KNOW WHO FAILED the counselling session, me or the earnest young woman on the other side of the desk. Her business card advertised her specialty as PTSD and anxiety disorders. I thought she looked too young for wisdom, the characteristic I most desire in a person who gives guidance.

In my quick-thinking way I sometimes make snap judgments about people that I'm always happy to be disabused of by a longer process of engagement. I hoped, as I sat down in the patient's chair, for a gentle abrasive weathering of my misgivings during the next sixty minutes.

We immediately got off on the wrong foot.

Instead of creeping up on the central issues, I came on like a scholar on speed, determined to show this woman I'd been reading papers at the leading edge of current research and suggesting, probably not very subtly, how she might approach my particular anxiety malfunction. When I drew breath she made a few notes then looked up at me with an unsteady gaze, like someone finding her balance after a heavy knock. In that brief exchange of eye contact I was sure she could never help me. If I had frightened her with one mildly manic outburst, how could she ever hope to get past the self-protective barriers I wear like body armour, or the verbal blinding-with-science chicanery I can put my tongue to when necessary?

She did what most people do when they're unsure or unsteady, she fell back on process. She picked up her pen again and asked me a set of questions she surely asks every client, carefully filling in the spaces and ticking a couple of boxes. I hoped that this stalling technique was a prelude to a sharp, insightful retort that would set me back on my heels. It was not. It was a form-filling exercise that was integral to her process. Her next move was to tell me that with trauma patients she employed a process of guided regression to the traumatic event, an induction of the original stressful feelings within the safe context of her watchfulness, then a guided procession back to the present.

These are not her words. I was so appalled I couldn't retain the actual speech. In the first instance, lady, I thought, I am not regressing anywhere with you. Public abreactions, weeping, breaking down in the arms of a watchful, caring counsellor – this is a place you will never find me. I do not role-play, or act out, or crumble and confess. I am not amenable to *gestalt*. And I am not going back to the darkness of the short-cut and a single rifle shot, not in your, or anybody else's, company.

I believe now that I showed this woman my worst side in order to provoke her best come-back. I wanted to know if I was putting myself in the hands of a wise and skilled healer who could see beyond the bluff and bluster.

Like all therapists, she kept an eye on the time, and as the hour drew to its end she went to a filing cabinet. What she brought back sent me into another stratosphere of angry resentment. On the desk she laid a photocopied sheet of cartoon drawings with annotations, depicting facial expressions associated with anxiety. The sheet helpfully told me that stress makes your heart race, your chest feel tight, your breathing become shallow. On the second page it outlined a deep breathing exercise. I looked at her to see if this was some sort of in-joke. I used to give out sheets like that to first-year high school science students, the ones who hadn't quite made the cognitive transition from pictures to words.

Ten minutes earlier I'd been genuinely asking if she'd seen the report from *Science* journal in which Israeli scientists had discovered a 'rogue cousin' of the brain chemical AchE-S. This rogue replaces the normal transmitter and disrupts signals travelling between nerve cells, and *might* point to a pathway by which people with PTSD over-react to everyday 'benign' fears. It was a mouse-brain study, but looked promising.

In the space of ten minutes we'd travelled from mouse brain to no brain.

The following day I rang my sister, who is a retired therapist.

After listening to me rant, she paused in that way trained listeners do and said, 'Oh Gail, you're such a snob.'

'*I am not*,' I bellowed. 'I went looking for help and was given a wonderword puzzle, *in big print*!'

But we kicked it around a bit and agreed that short of strapping gelignite to my armour plating, there wasn't much value in me pursuing the kind of therapy I was offered. 'There are other ways,' she said. '*You'll find them*.'

She reminded me of the time I'd consulted her in 1996 for help with fear of flying.

'I used a technique I keep in reserve for clients with strong ego defences.'

Try as I might, I couldn't recall what we'd done, only that it worked and didn't involve me weeping on her shoulder.

'I whisked you straight to your destination, *zoom*, you were in New Delhi waiting for your luggage at the carousel. This was the first image I gave your brain to tackle. Then we got into the sights and sounds of India. Once I had your higher brain occupied I kept it busy with challenges: what if this, what if that. When you felt comfortable and in control we started to backtrack, paying no attention to any fear signals. Eventually we got all the way back to Sydney airport.'

'Did we?' I said, my usually crisp recall not working.

'It took a couple of sessions.'

—

I thought back to 1983 when a Jungian analyst helped me leave my husband. She didn't know (or maybe she did) that my agenda was as cold-blooded as that, but I recall how readily, how happily, I wrote out my dreams and, later, how gladly I handed in my pages for the analyst's inspection. It was like poetry appreciation, like taking apart sonnets looking for meaning and art. There was often great beauty in the simplest of sentences. And strong visual pictures that lingered. And the bonus of ambiguity, the click of discovery.

Of course, I now realise, dream interpretation is a variant of narrative therapy, the variant that deals in the currency of the unconscious mind, and another method I am amenable to.

Since the advent of brain mapping machines, we can see which parts of the brain light up during the dreaming state. And, conversely, the bits that remain idle. For instance, the prefrontal cortex, where we do our conscious thinking and reality checking remains switched off. Anything goes in dreaming. The censors and thought police take the night off.

Other areas glow, depending on the content of what we dream. If there is colour and action and spectacular sights, the visual cortex switches on. If we are churning through highlights of the day's events, the hippocampus lights up. The pathways between the brainstem and the hearing and seeing areas pulse to create a sense that the dream is something that is really happening.

Nightmares, however, arrive on the heated dragon's breath of the amygdala.

In 1983 I wrote out dreams in which, among the dross,

certain themes recurred. Paying the price was one. I went through a lot of turnstiles (or arrived at shop counters, or was about to board a train) only to find my purse was empty, or I was a few pennies short of the fare. My analyst nodded her Viennese-trained head and told me to keep doing my dream work. Another dominant theme was 'taking my place'. If there was one seat left in a train carriage, I stood; one bed left in a hospital where I needed an operation, I dithered.

When we finished our sessions after a year I kept the diary going. But sporadically. Once my waking life was in some sort of order I got too involved in living to bother with reflection.

—

To my knowledge I've never dreamed about being shot. Nocturnal re-enactments have never been part of my pathology. Skimming through the dream diaries I see crazy visual scenes, and more prosaic snippets from my life as it was on that particular date. What stand out, if anything, are the occasional emissions of pure dread that rage at me like dangerous animals let out of a zoo. Fear dreams that are preverbal, or shape-suggestive, static from a malfunctioning beacon.

The residue from the shooting seems to have lodged in my limbic brain, nestled up to the fears (wherever they come from) that were there from a very long time ago. When I was ten or so, I was a sleepwalker. My parents spent weeks sleeping with one eye open after I walked from our house to the railway station one night. I was also a screamer, and still am. Out of a deep sleep I can suddenly sit up and wake the house with a piercing howl. Perhaps the bolts of electrical discharge are genetic (one of my sisters screams too). Perhaps they're existential.

IN EARLY 2002 when I was thinking about this book, I rented a house at Little Wobby, a small strip of cottages that look as if they fringe an island on the Hawkesbury River. The effect is deceiving. Leaving Brooklyn you catch a ferry which goes via Dangar Island, then approaches the jetty at Little Wobby. Coming in you see a single row of houses backing onto a high escarpment which might hide the rest of an island but which is in fact a headland projecting into the deep water (and good fishing) of the Hawkesbury.

My companion, Susan, another writer, and I had chosen this spot to work on our writing uninterrupted. It was an experiment in working independently of the writers' centres we'd both enjoyed in the past.

We were virtually alone at our end of the water-line. Down the other end, permanent residents caught the ferry to and from the mainland or took off in their own motorboats. Apart from the sounds of motorcraft, we heard gulls, and the clinking of moorings, and lazy water sounds.

We set up our workspaces to maximise the view (out of each other's line of sight) and organised the few domestic tasks we intended to do (like eating and drinking). I couldn't take my eyes off the view. My head dipped up and down all day.

It was one of the happiest weeks I've spent with my work. And mentally, one of the most perilous. Before leaving home I'd set myself the task of going back to the night I was shot, pushing myself into a vulnerable place to see how far I could go.

After so long not verbalising the shooting, not remembering detail, the venture had the potential for risk, as well as the potential for coming to nought. Short of self-hypnosis, I had no idea how one accesses what the brain has learnt to conceal.

The way the little house pressed its back into the escarpment pleased my need to sit in defensive postures, made me feel safe. I stayed in my nightgown and Chinese robe most of the day, staring at the glinting water, feeling as if I was on a liner at sea, mentally walking my seventeen-year-old self off the train, down the railway ramp and into the darkness. Lost in this meditation, I first remembered the *shove/kerwump* sensation, the doubt, the surprise, and the flash of red on the fireman's hand.

To gauge my progress I also began writing down dreams.

Clearly, my visual centres were operating.

A beach covered in snow. We approach a swelling, like a huge egg. It rises and cracks, yellow lava issues, runs into the waves. Streamers of lava lie parallel with the breaking waves. Great beauty. This is a daily event. We come as often as possible to watch.

As the week progressed the 'great beauty' diminished.

In the pharmacy. The prescription calls for a tall glass of warm water and suspended therein a pig's snout. Allow to stand. Decant the liquid. Patient to drink in one gulp.

Then –

A cat has been left in the sink. It has some sort of strange malady, a moving bulge, one minute the eye enlarges to bursting point, then its paw, then a grotesque pulsing lump moves in its neck like a diseased gland –

On the third night I woke myself with a scream and a madly pounding heart.

The next morning, I resumed staring at the water and thinking about the past. As a memory aid, I'd brought along a box of my oldest personal files. When I pulled out the notes and clippings from their homes in the piles of paper I can never seem to throw away, I found a sturdy cohesion of data, which, once sorted, took on the outline of a story. Without intending it, I'd been involved ever since I was shot in a long-term study of the effects of a single traumatic incident.

It was then that I recognised my desire to return to the scene of the crime as a *storyteller's impulse*. There is no mystery about the physical wound the gun inflicted. The mystery, the not knowing, relates to the other kind of damage the bullet caused.

My written responses to being shot were, at first, so minimal as to be almost non-existent. The diary entry 'Margot?' and the shark poem. My scrapbook has half a dozen newspaper clippings and some unconfiscated get-well cards. What I had saved was the context, the little souvenirs that placed me in a certain place at a given time. The Rolling Stones concert at the Sydney Showground 1966, an eighteenth birthday card, airline tickets, a Russian passenger ship menu. These are the pieces you slot in around the central event, the colour and movement that enriches a life.

I made random arrangements of these pieces of paper and hovered over them like the eagle I wanted to be as a child. The wind off the water blew the top layers about.

—

From the point of view of the observer, I see that what has been carried forward after so many years is not the total experience but the tics that developed in response to the experience, along with my coping responses to these tics. Put simply, I have coped by creating a safe, distanced narrative about what happened, one that avoids the emotional sinkholes, and a repertoire of tricks to fool my excitable brain into purposeful activity, a sort of mental picture-clearing by adjusting the fine control knobs.

And by self-medicating. I have never totally kicked my need for the little pills made by Roche. At university in the seventies we were told the story of Valium's discovery, how a young doctor got the idea from an animal trainer in a circus and talked a pharmaceutical company into marketing a tiger-taming potion for humans. I've used Valium to scare away the fear-tigers that interfere with my rest and growl inside my head when I need quiet, and I've also simultaneously held the idea that there is something inherently wrong with medicating what we don't understand or can't control. This is the dilemma of digging oneself into defensive positions.

Although I am not personally receptive to talking therapies (being a practised evader of face-to-face confession) I know that narrative therapies work by reconnecting portions of memory that have slipped their moorings and drifted apart. As we narrate, recount (and in my case), write, a magician steals in on tiptoes and sews up the broken threads. The longer we live, the more we tell, the smoother the peaks and troughs become: Unhappy childhood? Divorce? Shot? Beads on a string.

In 1986 I married again. I know I told my husband about being shot, but not straight away, and not in any emphatic, alerting way that would signal to him that there were issues ahead. As far as I knew the topic was a dead duck. I would guess that I told him in the slightly offhand way I'd developed of presenting the story, as if it were a novelty item tacked on to other episodes of my life before him. I would have located the old scrapbook, turned to the yellowing newspaper cuttings, and said, 'There I am, wasn't I young?'

—

When I was struck by a bullet in 1968 it was a bolt from the blue, as startling and monstrous as sniper fire is meant to be.

My world might have ended like that, on a dark road late at night, still in the greenness of my teenage life. Instead, my injuries healed, my shaken-up world view gradually realigned itself, and after a few months in the glow of extra attention, I reached out for the familiarity of my pre-shot life.

People who live after being shot often find themselves rerouted away from the normal path, always conscious that there is another road somewhere else, the one they should be on, the one that leads to safety. On this strange other-path they are often attacked and left helpless by phantoms and shadows that move. When they push through the undergrowth and regain the right path, they are elated by feelings of belonging and homecoming, and vow never to take their eyes off the signposts again.

But the inescapable truth is, there is no returning to the 'pre-shot' life, there is only 'after-shot' just as there is only after-war, after-rape, after-betrayal.

—

One evening last spring we were having dinner at a small Thai restaurant by the beach. It should have been a warm evening but a southerly change had hit about 5 pm and the air behind it was winter cool. I was leaning against the window looking out across the war memorial and park to the seawater streaming in from the ocean.

Out near the mouth of the bay, fishermen in yellow souwesters had positioned themselves to catch tailor on the turning tide. On the street beyond the window, people walked quickly to escape the chilly air. As we waited for our food I watched a family who'd stopped *en masse*, blocking the footpath while the mother pulled out windcheaters from a large backpack. The children hopped from foot to foot. The father seemed annoyed that this popular holiday spot had produced the wrong weather.

Just as my soup was set down I looked up once more to see the family move on and a couple take their place. The woman was small with a heart-shaped face. She wore a long black coat, collar turned up, over jeans. It was Wendy O'Shea with a friend.

A powerful zap went through me.

They checked out our restaurant, saw it was full, and went further down the road. That's Wendy, I wanted to say to anyone who would listen, that's the woman whose tragedy I've been immersed in, the woman I've been writing about. That woman, I wanted to say, *has been shot*.

I ignored the soup and watched Wendy read the menu posted on the door of the next restaurant. She checked with her companion, he shook his head, they went further. I told my husband, he looked out, couldn't see anyone and we started our meal. But the sentence wouldn't lie down. *That woman has been shot*.

I weighed the words in my head. A gunshot wound is like a branding mark; for a brief and painful time you are singled out, your flesh is sizzled, and then you return to the herd.

—

My accident was a private tragedy with no epic or heroic dimension, no meaning other than the obvious, no consequences other than the expected, yet glinting in the distance are some of the warning signs survivors of all tragedies glimpse. The loss of language to tell your story once you return from hell, the learning of silence when you've tried, no matter how understatedly, to describe your experience and in response been asked to keep your horrors to yourself, to stop frightening old people and children. The wilful forgetting. The act you perfect of fitting in again and being as you were before it all happened.

Since I opened that box of old papers, I've suffered an acuteness of the senses, and a consistent pain in my back, in an area roughly approximating the quadrant affected in the shooting. It's been a dull, subclinical manifestation, there but not there, both noticeable and endurable. Yoga has helped, so have the kneading hands of my physiotherapist.

I suspect it is a body memory, woken after thirty years out of its sleep of forgetting, to have its day in court. It may even be the track of my wound.

I can't make it go away by an act of will. I've tried.

—

On Tuesday evenings I work until 6 pm at a small pharmacy not far from home. Between 4 and 6 pm a girl called Alex works, for spending-money, after school. She's in her final year at high school and, at seventeen, is everything I felt I wasn't at her age. Clear-skinned, with big brown eyes, incredible eyelashes, not a touch of make-up and silky almost black hair that just touches her shoulders. She's studying Sylvia Plath for her HSC and we talk about poetry when we're not talking about her boyfriend or the latest staff scandal.

I'm older than Alex's mother, and sometimes I relate to her as if she's a borrowed daughter, but mostly I just enjoy being near the incandescence of her youth. One evening I had news of my own. I'd been to see the Rolling Stones at the Superdome and I raved breathlessly about being two rows from the stage (to the side, but nevertheless, *close*). I told her how I screamed when Mick Jagger looked straight into my eyes (no one else's) and how all the next day I floated around the house, singing to myself.

Coming out of my rave I saw her face trying to accommodate to this version of me she'd never seen. Half smiling, half puzzled, she stretched her big eyes into an expression of wonderment, and I kept going, describing the stage, the crowd, the atmosphere, as if I were bringing news from another country she would never visit.

Every closing time we go through a well-worn routine.

'It's a nice evening, I think I'll walk,' she says.

'Hop in,' I say, holding the passenger door open. Her house is only a few blocks away, maybe a ten-minute walk.

I've heard it all before: It's not far, It's her hometown, for heaven's sake, She needs the exercise.

I don't fill her head with horrors, even though I could point out that Anita Cobby, Janine Balding, Helen Harrison and a hundred others were all *just on their way home*.

My seventy-five-year-old mother is still doing this, bringing her children safely home. Every night before she goes to sleep she mentally puts each of us to bed. When any of us go away, even for a day, she is the first to ring. *Just checking, everything alright*?

I have driven many girls like Alex home over the years, sometimes miles out of my way, always over their protestations. They shine the laser lights of their youth and invincibility on the world out there and still only manage to see a few feet in front of their noses.

'Humour me,' I say, as I scoot them into my car.

Acknowledgements

This book was conceived as an exploration of the short- and long-term effects of being shot. It is a 'personal response', a category of written pursuit that implies subjectivity, but also includes, I hope, good sense and due respect for documented truths.

Individuals and references that have helped my understanding are mentioned in the text and any mistakes or misinterpretations are mine.

I began the writing by interrogating my own memories of being shot and could not have sustained that process without the good humour and sense of proportion of my husband, Andrew.

When I'd exhausted my own recollections I turned to my parents and siblings, who were with me in 1968 and have always been there for me. I dedicate the book to my late mother, Alice, for her vigilance and love, and all those nights of waiting up.

Longstanding friends – Pam Summers, Sue May, Kay Barton, R.H. – offered memories from the past; while other friends and contacts found information or made suggestions that steered my search in a useful direction; Brendan Donnellan, Jack Eckert, N. Feltis, Brendon Gordon, Kris Heke, Colleen Henry, Theo Hystek, Roger Johnson, Trish Marston, Philip McLaren, Dr W. Munro, Nicole, Dr Ameeta

Patel, Jan Raso, R. Shankelton, Terry Taylor and Bill Tibben.

The people who agreed to share their stories with me – Wendy O'Shea, Billy T., Mal Hundt, Lisa, Jean, Dennis and Brendon – are the heroes on these pages. I hope I've done justice to their trust in me.

Peter Bishop gave me his impressions of the book in draft stage and greatly encouraged the narrative choices I made through what was often difficult emotional terrain. Barbara Holloway and Simone Ford offered important comments; and Susan Hampton is a constant source of intelligent appraisal. And, finally, a huge thank you to Judith Lukin-Amundsen for applying her editorial laser beam to my prose.